Complex Characters

Bill Bynum

FLORIDA COLLEGE
PRESS

Complex Characters
Copyright © 2021
Florida College Press
Temple Terrace, Florida

Printed in the United States of America

ISBN: 978-1-736175-21-7

Contents

Introduction

Sometimes life is really complicated. We have so many decisions to make about things that really matter. We want to do what is right, and we want to do things that will end well. God has given us lots of tools to help us in our efforts. A look into the lives of some people who lived complex lives in their complex world is one of these tools. The stories recorded in the Bible are written not only to allow us to see God's overall plan for humanity, but also to let us look at how some of these people dealt with the really complicated issues they faced. Their experiences, both good and bad, provide examples for us to learn about what to do and not to do. Think about how often in the New Testament, especially in a text like Hebrews 11, the lives of different people are referenced. In other passages, like Romans 15:4 and 1 Corinthians 10:1, more general statements are made about learning from the lives of those who lived in the past. God expects us to know and use these.

Though these stories are there for us, we often do not benefit from them. These lessons will help us understand why we don't learn more from them as well as how to fix that problem. We "know" the stories. Some of us began learning them when we were quite young. However, the version of the stories we would have learned then were typically very simple, age-appropriate, and incomplete. While it was great at the time, the stuff left out was often the information that would show the complexity of their circumstances and allow us a greater opportunity to learn from their lives. In the past when we studied the lives of people in the Bible, it was typically a one-dimensional approach that painted them as good or bad with very broad strokes. It's not that simple. On those frequent occasions when God chose to provide enough data for us to see the complexity of the people and their world, he did so for a reason. Part of that is so we can learn from them.

Their complex stories touch our hearts and show us characters to whom we can relate. When we gloss over their uncertainties, struggles, and even failures we lose our ability to relate to them. When we can't relate to them, they lose much of their ability to inspire or warn us. Also, when we gloss over certain parts of their lives, we show a lack of care in our approach to the scriptures. That is a big deal in every way.

How does this happen? Sometimes it happens because we only know a slice of the story, but think we know all of it. Other times, for the sake of simplicity or brevity, we skip details that actually make a huge difference. Sometimes there are very significant people we have never studied at all. There may even be characters that since we have preconceived ideas about them being good or bad, we subconsciously gloss over the information that contradicts our conclusions.

Well, that's the problem. How do we fix it? We fix it by going back and looking at some of these stories that we probably imagine we already know. When you saw some of the lesson titles, you may have thought, "I already know that story!" Even if that is the case, I think you will be surprised at what you learn. That includes not only the information you learn about their lives, but also how it helps you in a very practical way in your life. When we look at these stories, we aren't going to leave out the information about their hard choices, conflicted intentions, lack of understanding, and frequent failures. We aren't approaching it this way to pick on them or mess up your heroes, but so we can be careful students who learn from the information God has chosen to provide. As we examine these details, we will think about how these impacted their decision-making process, the outcomes they experienced in their lives, and the ramifications in the lives of others. That will allow us to take the next step of thinking about similar, at least in concept, circumstances we face and how to make choices that will please God, be good for us, and help others. Please remember, the real answers that help us with our complex lives in this complex world come from God through his word (Jeremiah 10:23, Ps 119:9-11).

The characters we will study exemplify the fact that God can and does use a variety of "real" people to accomplish his purposes. This should help us marvel even more at his love and power as well as encourage and motivate us to rise above our challenges to serve the Lord as best we can.

Questions

1. How many specific names of Bible characters can you find in Hebrews 11? (This isn't "busy work." It's a trick to get you to actually spend some time looking at that chapter.)

2. Do we have the wisdom in ourselves to direct our lives? What will help us recognize and avoid sin?

3. Who are some Bible characters we think of as always being "good" and not really struggling?

4. Who are some Bible characters we think of as being simply and purely "bad?"

Match the person with the story

Joseph	Needed to be protected from pride
Gideon	Stole the family idols
Paul	Was a tattle-tale
Manasseh	Laughed at God's promise
Rachel	Repented and was blessed
Sarah	Told Jesus "no."
Samson	Accomplished more in death than in life
Peter	Stole the family idols

For Discussion

1. Is it difficult to learn from the life of someone who we imagine never had any struggles, uncertainties, or problems? Why?

2. Is it difficult to learn from someone we only think of as a "bad" person? Why?

3. Details matter. Have there been times in your life when if more details had been known the story would have appeared to be quite different?

Sarah

Before you read this chapter or the Biblical texts, share what you remember about Sarah. Include factual details as well as impressions of her character.

Her name meant princess, and that she was. She played such a prominent role in the Bible story that she is familiar to most of us. Her life was made complex by many things. She left her home and family in what would have been a cosmopolitan city of Ur to live a nomadic life with her husband Abraham. For much of her married life she dealt with the stigma and disappointment of being barren. Because of her great and enduring beauty, she felt danger in some of the places they temporarily lived. Following the customs of the time, her servant produced a child with her husband, and this, in turn, created stress in the family. (Imagine that!) During all of this, she lived with the fact that her husband had been made promises by God that were absolutely mind-boggling but unfolded seemingly quite slowly. Her story was truly complex as she lived in a complex world.

This class

- Reminds us of the story
- Examines some of the complexities of the story
- Shows us the applications we should make

The Story We Know

Abraham and Sarah listened to God and left their home for the land of promise. God had promised them the land, innumerable descendants, protection, and to be the conduit through whom one of their descendants would be a blessing to the entire world.

Much of this promise was predicated on them having a child. It's really hard to be the parents of a great nation when you don't have any kids. While there are other subplots like Lot and Sodom and Gomorrah, most of the story is connected to their dealing with God's promise of a child that took a number of years to be fulfilled.

As they waited and traveled, God continued to speak with them to assure them. Just a year before their child was to be born, God appeared to them and told them the time was near. This posed a challenge to their faith since they were biologically past the point of having a child together. Their faith demonstrated itself as they resumed the necessary physical intimacy for a child to be produced.

Along the way, following a common custom in the ancient near east, Abraham fathered a child who could legally be considered the offspring of both Abraham and Sarah. However, after that, she gave birth to a son. Sarah rejoiced when her child was born and celebrated by saying that with the birth of Isaac (Laughter) those who had laughed at her will now laugh with her. (Gen. 21:6-7) After he was born to Sarah and Abraham, the servant and her son Ishmael were sent away under God's protection.

She lived about 36 more years before dying and being buried with great honor.

Though not often mentioned outside of Genesis, it is clear from other references that she was a person of faith. Despite the textual challenge of Hebrews 11:11, it seems clear that she is included as one of the heroes of faith in that chapter. She is also invoked as an example of a godly wife in 1 Peter 3:6.

It's a beautiful and fascinating story, and it's much more complex than either the above or typical telling of it. Let's explore some of that. As we do this, we will focus on five episodes that the text call special attention to. These episodes show much about Sarah's character. She had strong self-preservation and maternal instincts. She was not simply a quiet, always compliant person who was unwilling to express strong feelings. On multiple occasions she demonstrated a very strong personality. None of these things are bad, but as we shall see, each contains the potential for problems.

In Egypt

Upon their arrival into the promised land it seemed more like a "famine land." They chose, as others would after them, to go to Egypt for food. The text uses a term that suggests they were planning on staying there (12:10). Sarah's beauty created a perceived danger that resulted in fear trumping faith when they deceived the Pharaoh about her relationship to Abraham (12:12-13).

This "defiled rather than death" mentality resulted in Sarah being taken into Pharaoh's house as a wife (12:15,19). Verse 16 may represent the bride price he paid her actual husband for her. Perhaps it was Sarah who explained the connection between the deceit and the plague that afflicted Egypt which led to them being kicked out of the land. Their circumstances were new and perhaps understandably scary, but the way they chose to deal with it resulted in Sarah being taken as another man's wife, great suffering in Egypt. It also showed a lack of faith.

"Helping Out"

About 10 years after the initial promise, Sarah decided to help things along. She blamed God for the fact that she has not been able to conceive (16:2) and suggested an alternative. She had an Egyptian slave (perhaps part of her bride price) that she decided should bear a child for her (16:2). As strange as this sounds to us, it was a culturally accepted and legally recognized means of securing an heir throughout the ancient Near East. The man was seen as providing all that was needed for the child while the woman was essentially an incubator. Our feeling that she is overstepping bounds appears verified by a subtly used parallel. The wording of "took," "gave," and "accepted" is distinctly related to that found in Genesis 3:17. The child that was produced did not represent faith by the "flesh" (Gal. 4:29).

The plan "works" in that Hagar does become pregnant. The problems caused by the inherently flawed plan soon became apparent. Hagar, now carrying Abraham's child, experienced a loss of respect for her master. Maybe she imagined her position within the family changing, and as an Egyptian never liked the idea of being the slave of a nomadic family. Sarah, perhaps driven by second thoughts or jealousy treats Hagar so harshly that she flees towards home. While her child was not to be the child of promise, her child did receive a wonderful promise. Notice throughout this section she is painted in a generally favorable light, while Sarah's treatment of her is described as "harsh" and as her having "afflicted" Hagar.

Laughing

An extended period elapses before God approaches them again about the promised child. During this gap, Hagar's son Ishmael grows to be a teenager, and Abraham passes the point in life of being naturally able to father a child (See Heb. 11:12 and Rom. 4:17) In Genesis 17, God repeats the promise to Abraham assuring him that Sarah will be a mother (Gen. 17:19). Subsequent to this, the Lord and two angels arrive at Abraham's home to announce that within a year the child will be born. Sarah is involved in the proper hospitality but conceals herself by staying inside the tent during the ensuing conversation. Though inside, she has positioned herself in a place to be able to overhear (eavesdrop?) what is said (Gen. 18:10). Upon hearing that she will have a child, she laughs. At some point, she joins the conversation and is challenged for her laughter. She lies about having laughed, and her lie is corrected. The details of her amusement are not given, but surely included the idea that she and Abraham, as an old couple, would resume their physical intimacy (Gen. 18:12). The fact that they did so was a part of their demonstration of faith in God's promise.

Again!?

The events involving Abimelech occurred during a time when Sarah was already pregnant or trying to become pregnant. In Genesis 20, Abraham and Sarah again lie about their relationship out of fear. On a practical level, the stakes are higher this time. A repeat of what had happened in Egypt would put the parentage of Sarah's child in question. To prevent this, all of the women connected to Abimelech were prevented from becoming pregnant. Also, God spoke to Abimelech to warn him not to have relations with the already married Sarah. In a scene where the righteousness of Abimelech clearly outshines that shown by Abraham and Sarah, Abraham explains their rationale. It isn't impressive. He seems to say, "God makes me travel to all these dangerous places, so we always misrepresent our relationship wherever we go. Coming to be around godless people such as yourself made it necessary again" (Gen. 20:13). While their fear might have been understandable the first time, now it isn't. They have experienced years of God's faithfulness to his promise to bless those who bless them and curse those who curse them, yet they doubt his protection and bring harm on the innocent.

Expelling the Rivals

During the celebration of Isaac being weaned, Sarah witnessed the teenaged Ishmael laughing at Isaac. The wording leaves the nature of this interaction very unclear with the possibilities ranging from innocent interaction to cruel mockery. At this point, she verbalized fears about which would be the actual heir (Gen. 21:10) and demanded that Hagar and Ishmael be driven away from the family. Abraham is loathe to do so, but God instructs him to go along with Sarah's wishes and assures him that the mother and child will be cared for. Sarah's attitude and demands are not vindicated simply by virtue of that fact they coincide with God's plan. Once again strife which originated from the choice to "help" God has been brought into the family.

As a closer look at the text has highlighted, Sarah was a complex person trying to navigate some very complex circumstances. While we can learn from her successes and strengths, we can learn even more from her struggles.

Lessons

Throughout the story, we see that God keeps his promises regardless of whatever else was going on. He was protecting Abraham and Sarah and bringing consequences on those who would do them harm. Looking back at the differences between how the situation with Pharaoh and Abimelech played out seems to reflect this idea.

The story shows much about faith. Faith is something that grows and matures over time as God's people see his power and faithfulness. At the same time, it has opportunities to be tested when things are difficult.

Throughout the story we have seen times when Abraham and Sarah would have been better off to have sought God's word and waited patiently for him. Moving to Egypt, lying about their relationship, and using Hagar as a surrogate all seem to be examples of this.

God doesn't need our "help." We need to trust in him and do his will.

Jealousy and blaming others for our mistakes poisons any relationship, especially within a family.

Questions

1. List the promises made in Genesis 12:1-3. How do you see these being fulfilled throughout this story?

2. What are some of the key personality traits you see Sarah displaying?

3. How do you reconcile what you see from her in Genesis with how she is described in 1 Peter 3:6?

4. Does she seem to be oversensitive? If so, what might have contributed to this?

5. To what degree do you believe Sarah was complicit with the lying? Was she really his half-sister?

6. Show the parallels between Genesis 16:2 and Genesis 3:17.

7. Given her age, what might account for Sarah being so attractive?

Discussion

1. Does God need our "help?" How does it usually work out when we try?

2. What does the text tell us about what Hagar experienced and how she felt (Chapters 16 and 21)? What details show her in a positive light?

3. How did Sarah's personality traits identified in this text create potential problems for her?

4. Discuss the dishonesty we saw on a couple of occasions. Be sure to include the fact they were half-siblings.

Rachel

I don't know who first said "family is messy," but it would surely have applied to the family of Isaac. The Jacob and Esau conflict was bad enough, but when you throw in Jacob's relationship with Laban's family, it takes messy to another level. We will try to extricate one character from this veritable buffet of complexities to examine. Rachel is often seen as a heroine of faith as well as a character from a great love story. Let's carefully examine the text to see what we can learn about her life and from her life.

The Story We Know

To ensure that Jacob did not marry a Canaanite, Isaac sent him to find a wife from among his cousins (Gen. 28:1). (This also wisely put some distance between Jacob and Esau.) Upon arriving, he met Rachel who was helping care for the flocks. Though his strong display of emotion on that occasion was surely more complex, it surely included him being attracted to her as a potential bride (Gen. 29:11,18). Rachel's father, Laban, agreed to allow Jacob to work for seven years in exchange for Rachel as a wife. When the time arrived for the marriage to occur, Leah was treacherously substituted in Rachel's place. This was not discovered until after the marriage and its consummation. As odd as this may seem, a combination of factors including darkness, a desire to be relatively quiet with family nearby, and wine from the marriage feast probably help to explain it (Gen. 29:25).

When the deceit was discovered and Jacob expressed his displeasure, Laban agreed to allow him to go ahead and marry Rachel as well in exchange for seven more years of labor (Gen. 29:27). For a variety of reasons which probably included the fact Rachel was more physically attractive, resentment over being tricked, and working seven additional years, Rachel was Jacob's favorite wife, and this preference manifested itself (Gen. 29:30-31). This relationship and the rivalry that developed was played out in the producing of children with Jacob. Rachel, unable to conceive herself, provided her servant Bilhah to Jacob in hopes that Bilhah would have a child. The competition for children between Leah and her servant versus Rachel and her servant resulted in many children for Jacob. Not only did Bilhah produce children, but God allowed Rachel to give birth to two sons as well. She died during the birth of the second son (Gen. 35:17-19).

During this period, God told Jacob it was time for his growing family to leave Laban (Gen. 31:3). The financial arrangements between the two became complex and filled with treachery to the extent that Jacob decided to sneak away with his family and possessions (Gen. 31:20-21). As she made preparations to leave, Rachel stole the household idols and concealed them (Gen. 31:34-35). When confronted by her father, she avoided search and successfully deceived him by claiming she was having her period.

This is surely a messy story that really doesn't leave us identifying any of the characters in a great light. Digging deeper into the complexities of the story will help us understand more about why things happened and what we can learn from the story, especially Rachel's role in it.

Let's begin by looking a little more closely at one aspect of her life and two specific events. To put these into context, we need some background. Laban's family was closely connected to the family of promise, but they were not the people of promise worshiping the one true God. Their idols were obviously very important to them. Rachel grew up with a father who was quite willing to be duplicitous in his dealings with anyone around him. As a wife, she watched intrigue and treachery play out between her husband and father. Also, she married into a family where preferential treatment and deceit were not unknown. Did she know Jacob's story, including not only his role in the process of receiving the birthright but also of the blessing? Did she know he was in fear for his life from his brother? All of this would have had an impact on her attitude and behavior.

She also lived in a time when success as a wife was inextricably connected to producing children. Sons especially provided a mother with status and security. As a numbers game, for the nation promise to be fulfilled, the family needed to start growing quickly. Jacob took care of that. The awkward and unfortunate family dynamics created by polygamy were relatively new to the family. Hagar not-withstanding, Abraham's wife was Sarah till her death. Isaac was married to Rebekah. Multiple sister-wives and their servants were bound to be problematic.

Stealing the Idols

Genesis 31:34-35 tells us that as they were leaving Laban's terri-tory, Rachel stole the household idols. Put into context, that isn't so surprising. Lying, tricking, and stealing seem to have been the norm in her environment. She felt that her father had stolen from her (Gen. 31:14-16). This was likely a reference to the bride price not being properly paid or preserved for the sisters.

Why did she steal the idols? She came from a pagan family. She probably believed in the power of the idols. Notice in chapter 35:2-4 they still had and valued them. The idols probably also had eco-nomic value. There is also the possibility that possessing the idols gave control over who became the heir. It might be that Rachel imagined having them would allow Jacob to return to her home after her father died and supplant her oldest brother. It's more likely that she imagined it would give her son priority over her sister's oldest son. Of course, none of this excuses her behavior, but it helps us better understand why she did what she did.

Rivalry Over Children

Genesis 29:31 tells us that Leah was blessed with the ability to conceive but Rachel was not. Her response to the birth of four sons is to credit and praise the Lord for his graciousness. Rachel's response was two-fold. She envied her sister and blamed Jacob for her failure to conceive (Gen. 30:1). This envy coupled with her pouty blaming of Jacob and saying she will just die if she doesn't have a child isn't a pretty picture. Verse 8 of the chapter demonstrates that her focus wasn't on the well-being of the family, but on her competition with her sister. For her, family was a zero-sum game (See Vv. 14-16 of the same chapter). Only later, in verse 22, do we see her reaching out to God, being heard, and being blessed with her son Joseph. Why did she act like this? Bearing a son was culturally and practically important. Her own family dynamic had been all about doing whatever it took to get ahead, even if it meant mistreating family. In addition to her own experience, did she know about what had happened in Jacob's family with deceiving Isaac to take priority? Was she frightened about her own future if she failed to produce children? All of that is very possible, but as the final event will seemingly suggest, she was a selfish person.

Birth of Benjamin

In Genesis 35 we are told that she became pregnant again. However, there were complications with the pregnancy that resulted in her death. (There is a darkly ironic connection between this and 30:1.) The risk of death in childbirth was much greater in the ancient world than in the modern western world. Before she died, the mid-wife sought to comfort her by assuring her she had given birth to a son. Her response was to name the child "son of my sorrow." Thankfully, rather than allowing the tragedy of this naming to stand, Jacob named him "son of my right hand."

As we look at her life as a whole, it isn't surprising that she is not held up as a model of faith by Biblical writers. In fact, she is only mentioned once in the New Testament, and that is not a statement about her character. Regardless of how her life should be assessed, it surely provides an opportunity to learn from vital lessons for our complex lives in this complex world.

Lessons

Rachel, like many today, was surrounded by many negative influences and bad examples. Often when this is the case, the choice is made to reflect the values of the environment and use that as an excuse for bad behavior. That's the wrong approach. If we are surrounded by bad things, we need to recognize them, be aware of the dangers those influences pose in our lives, and determine to, by the grace of God, rise above these challenges. Rather than allowing what's going on around us to pull us down, we need to see the damage and dangers of the bad and allow that to motivate us to do better.

Walter Scott wrote, "O, what a tangled web we weave when first we practise to deceive!" Dishonesty begets additional dishonesty. When people start lying, cheating, and stealing it becomes difficult to stop. Often additional dishonesty is chosen to hide the previous. A lack of trust wreaks havoc on relationships. Imagine how little trust existed among the people in the story of Rachel. People often begin lying to themselves in an effort to justify their actions. While our society has trivialized honesty, it is something God takes very seriously (Prov. 6:17, Rev. 21:8).

Polygamy was tolerated and regulated by God for a time, but it was never his intent. When he created man and woman, he made them in a way that optimized their ability to complement one another in a monogamous lifelong relationship which would produce children. Any deviation from that comes with problems. Jacob's family dynamics provide a detailed, unpleasant illustration of this. It does harm to everyone involved. Complex families have become the norm in our society, but that doesn't mean it is right or good. We need to dedicate ourselves to acknowledging God's plan for family, striving for that in our lives, honestly recognizing the problems that failure causes, and being compassionate with those who find themselves in unfortunate situations.

Questions

1. Was it "love at first sight" for Jacob and Rachel?

2. What seemed to impress Jacob about Rachel (Gen. 29:17-18)? Is this important? Is it the most important thing?

3. Discuss the naming of the children. What does the process suggest about the character of each sister?

4. What shows how important the idols were to both Laban and Rachel?

5. How does this story fit into the big picture of God fulfilling his promises to Abraham?

Discussion

1. Do you see anything in the story that might suggest Rachel struggled with both gratitude and a sense of entitlement?

2. Define "honesty." How would you explain the concept of a "partial truth?" Give examples of how people can be dishonest in the context of work or school.

3. After reading this story, whose character impressed you in a positive way? How do you feel about Leah? Why?

Joseph

His is a story we have known well for a long time. Or have we? He has certainly been the topic for many Bible classes and sermons. We have a lot of information about him. He is a major player in more than a third of the long book of Genesis. This huge amount of material allows us to trace his life from his childhood to his death, and from a prisoner/slave till he became one of the most powerful men in the world. He was a hero who was compelled to navigate incredibly complex circumstances in his complex world. He did it well, but not without some challenges and missteps along the way. Let's look at the story and try to do so as if we have never read or heard it before to see what his life was really like and what we can learn from it. You may be surprised by what we find.

At Home

From his earliest mention, it is clear that he was special. He was loved by his parents, though apparently, at least in the case of the father, not so much because of his virtues but because he was the child of Jacob's old age (Gen. 37:3). It was also apparent that he would play a major role in God's plan for keeping his promises to Joseph's grandfather, Abraham.

From the text of Genesis 15:13-16, we see that several things had to happen before Abraham's descendants would possess the promised land.

1. They needed to leave the promised land. Something big would have to cause that.

2. They needed to go to Egypt specifically.

3. They needed to grow greatly numerically while not assimilating.

4. Somehow, they needed to be oppressed, but also get kicked out.

Joseph would play a key role in these things happening.

While Joseph had a huge role to play, and his father loved him more than his other children, he was not a likable kid. Part of that was not his fault, but part of it was. It wasn't his fault that his father made him a special coat that showed his preferred status, but it was his choice to wear it to go find his brothers in the field (Gen. 37:23). It was also his fault that he would bring a "bad report" about the brothers to their father. The Hebrew word that is translated "report" is consistently used in a negative way towards the one speaking (Num. 13:32, 14:36-37), and is qualified by "bad." At the very least he was a tattletale, and was most likely, based on the meaning of this phrase, making up or embellishing the facts to get his brothers in trouble.

Joseph's dreams (Gen. 37:5-11) played a key role in providing early insight into his significant place in the future of the family, but his handling of these dreams also contributed to the hatred he experienced from his brothers. Apparently, this included a couple of different things. The verb tense in verse 9 suggests that he was continually telling his brothers about the dreams, and he seemed to be not only telling what he saw in the dreams, but providing the interpretation that his family would bow down to him in such a way that even his doting father finally strongly reprimanded him (Gen. 37:10).

These issues all seemed to converge in a tragic way when Joseph, wearing the coat that indicated he was the favorite, traveled to check up on his brothers on behalf of their father. Their anger boiled over to the extent that the discussion began with "let's kill him." This moderated as they decided to "only" sell him to slave traders who would take him far from his home and family (Gen. 37:18-35).

Slave and Prisoner

During the incredibly difficult days and years that followed, it is impossible for us to say for sure what all helped to sustain Joseph. Perhaps, at least for a while, it was hope that his father would come and rescue him. That hope would have faded. It surely included his cognizance of God and belief that there was something special in store for him, and that God would keep the promises made to the fathers (Heb. 11:22). In each key part of his story, we see him making choices based on God's will and giving God the credit for what he was able to do.

He was purchased by a top army official named Potiphar as a household slave. The Lord blessed his efforts to do well, and perhaps he had functioned in some supervisory capacity at home despite his youth. Because of his character and work ethic, he was put in charge of the household (Gen. 39:4). His master's wife tried repeatedly to seduce Joseph, but he continued to resist until the last time when she tried to force him, and as a result, he ran and left her holding his garment (Gen. 39:12). Her anger at this rejection led her to accuse Joseph of attempted rape. The text leaves us to wonder at whom the suspicion and anger of Potiphar was directed, but it was Joseph who was put into prison.

Again, the Lord blessed him and his efforts to do well, and that resulted in him being put in charge there also (Gen. 39:23). Two personal servants of the king who had been imprisoned by him and placed in the care of Joseph had dreams. God, through Joseph, interpreted those dreams, and Joseph asked the one who was to be restored to service to tell the king of his plight. Sadly, perhaps in his joy at his own good fortune, he forgot (Gen. 40:23).

Elevated

Two years later, Pharaoh had dreams so troubling that he was determined to have them explained. This prompted the cupbearer's memory, and he told Pharaoh about Joseph (Gen. 41:9-13). Upon being summoned, Joseph explained the dreams and the role God was playing in it (Gen. 41:25,32). During this explanation, Joseph made some preliminary suggestions about how to deal with the upcoming years of plenty and the following years of famine (Gen. 41:33-36). Consequently, he was made the second most powerful person in the kingdom at the age of 30 (Gen. 41:46).

With Family Again

The famine's impact led to 10 of his brothers traveling to Egypt to buy food. When these foreigners appeared before their brother, they did not recognize him (Gen. 42:8). He had grown from a boy into a man, and both his grooming and dress would have been quite different than theirs. The following series of conversations during multiple encounters with his brothers were complex and, in some ways, a little difficult to evaluate. This included a series of questions and demands to test them that allowed Joseph to learn about the state of his father and his brother Benjamin. No doubt in addition to wondering if his father was still alive, he was curious about any efforts that might have been made to search for him after his disappearance. (Remember, he did not know about the "killed by a wild animal" story.) Surely, he also wondered if, with his absence, Benjamin, who was the other favored son, might have experienced the wrath of the brothers.

This process, as well as the information it generated, would also have given him an opportunity to assess the character of his brothers to see if they were fundamentally good men who cared about their family. Throughout this process of interviewing and bringing the family, there are multiple occasions where he employed deceit. The most obvious and troubling of these was found in the first part of Genesis 44. As a part of the ruse to accuse his brothers of theft they were not guilty of, Joseph had his servant tell the brothers that part of what they had stolen was the cup with which he practiced divination. This leaves us a bit uncertain as to whether he was having his servant lie about the cup or he really did practice divination. Either way, it seems to remind us that in spite of his amazing faith, he was an imperfect man.

His handling of all of this may seem a bit insensitive, and to some degree it was. It surely caused his father a great deal of additional worry. Maybe the years of people disappointing and failing him had left him a bit cynical about human nature. However, in the process of this, he decided to invite the family to come to Egypt and probably felt a responsibility to know what kind of people he was inviting.

At the end of this process, in a beautiful and emotional scene, Joseph revealed himself to his brothers. Understandably, they were filled with guilt and fear. The process Joseph put them through had forced them to relive what they had done to him and the impact it had had on their father. Joseph assured them, both at that time and later when their father died and their fears returned, that he would not seek vengeance against them. While acknowledging that they had done evil, he explained that God had used it for good (Gen. 50:20).

Sidebar

Another fascinating aspect of the story was the sweeping economic changes that Joseph's policies brought to the land. These, summarized, included, essentially the end of private property in Egypt with even the people becoming slaves (Gen. 47:13-25).

Family in Egypt

Joseph brought the family into the land and secured for them the pasture land of Goshen where they thrived until the death of Joseph and the Pharaoh that he had served.

Lessons

There are so many lessons we can learn from this incredibly complex story. While most are from his tremendous demonstrations of faith, some of them are from his failures. Let's look at a summary of some of these.

When we are blessed with amazing blessings and opportunities, we need to accept and use them with humility. Flaunting them will create resentment. While each person is accountable for his own attitudes and actions, we need to be aware that our behavior can contribute to the errors of others.

When we are mistreated, we cannot allow ourselves to blame God and give up. We need to do the best we can in the circumstances in which we find ourselves. That includes caring about the well-being of others. The dream discussion with Pharaoh's servants began with Joseph noticing that the men were troubled (Gen. 40:6). Had he been totally self-absorbed, the conversation that resulted in Pharaoh hearing about his ability to interpret dreams would never have occurred.

We need to always remember that God is in control and uses his power to accomplish his purposes. That will often include the evil that people choose to do.

Joseph realized that he was not in the place of God to punish his brothers (Gen. 50:19). We need to remember the same thing. He was, despite the terrible things he suffered, willing to truly forgive. We must be willing to do so as well.

Questions

1. Briefly explain the role Joseph played in the things that needed to happen before the Israelites would possess the promised land.

2. How did Jacob's treatment of Joseph contribute to the hatred that the others felt for him?

3. Against whom did Joseph say adultery would have been a sin?

4. What experiences in management and administration did Joseph have that may have helped prepare him for the task Pharaoh gave him?

5. From your reading of the text, why did Joseph test his brothers as he did?

Discussion

1. Have you ever felt that another family member was "the favorite?" Was it necessarily their fault? How did you overcome it to treat everyone fairly?

2. How would Joseph's handling of the dreams help create the hatred his brothers felt? Can you think of a better way he might have handled this?

3. Try to imagine the processes of being SOLD by your siblings and PURCHASED by a stranger. How would you feel? With whom all might you be angry?

4. Can you remember any time in your life when some "bad" experience was necessary to get you where you needed to be? Did Joseph experience this?

5. Joseph could have easily felt sorry for himself, vowed to do as little as possible, and waited for rescue. How do you think things would have worked out for him had he not done his best to excel in the different circumstances in which he found himself?

6. Is it fair to want to see that someone who has mistreated us has actually changed before we trust them again?

Gideon

"Wait! No, not Gideon. We 'know' the story, and it's a simple and good one. He does not belong in this book!" It's understandable if you are feeling this way. It is a story you may have been hearing all of your life as a good, positive, upbeat, simple story that ended with everyone living happily ever after. Truthfully, it's more complex.

The Story You May Know

In the days of the judges when the Midianites were oppressing Israel, an angel appeared to Gideon to call him to be a deliverer. His humble response to the messenger included worshiping the Lord. As commanded, he proceeded to tear down an altar to Baal and build an altar to God. The Spirit of the Lord was enabling him, and he mustered the people to war. 32,000 answered the call. Because the number was so great, God put them through a winnowing process to reduce the numbers so significantly that when the battle was over, there could be no doubt that God gave the victory. With his band of 300, he worshiped God and was assured victory. They attacked with an odd assortment of weapons, shouting, "a sword for the Lord and for Gideon." The Lord gave them an overwhelming victory that ended the Midianite threat.

All of that is true; it can be read in Judges 6:21-7:22. Yet, that version is one dimensional and leaves out such a great amount of critically important information that it leaves us with a false sense of the story. It's an incredibly complex story, and in many ways it ends badly. Let's start with the clearly bad ending and work our way back through other bad elements and try to find the source of the problem.

The Story We May Not Know

"And Gideon made an ephod of it and put it in his city, in Ophrah. And all Israel whored after it there, and it became a snare to Gideon and to his family." (Judges 8:27, ESV)

That is clearly and completely bad. At best, he was the wrong person to build something like this, and Ophrah was the wrong place for a cultic site. He wasn't even a Levite, and that was not where God had authorized worship. This ephod (perhaps a golden image made in the form of the priestly garment) led to nation-wide, home-grown idolatry that paved the way for the return of an even more virulent strain of Baal worship.

There were other problems from the post-victory period of his life as well. We aren't told how many wives and concubines he had, but we do know he had 70 sons. One concubine was a Canaanite from Shechem (8:31). His son by this woman, Abimelech, made himself a king by force and in the process murdered his male siblings (9:5). Where did he get the idea of becoming king? Perhaps from his father when he named him Abimelech which means "my father is the king." Why would he have given his son that name? Let's go back a bit further.

In 8:22, we see the men of Israel offering to make Gideon a dynastic king. They made the offer based on the premise that Gideon had saved them from Midian. They made this error despite the fact that the entire story made it clear that the great victory of Midian was from God (7:2, 22). This would have been a really good time for Gideon to have reminded them to give God the glory, but he didn't. He did verbally refuse the offer (8:23), but his actions looked a whole lot more like he accepted the offer and reigned. He:

- Took kingly spoils of war (7:24-25)
- Executed what was at best royal privilege in dealing with cities east of the river (8:14-17)
- Took royal symbols from the Midianite kings (8:26)
- Created a cultic center/capitol (8:27)
- Had a kingly harem (8:30-31)
- Named his son Abimelech (8:31)

Why Did it End This Way?

This was a bad ending of the story for Gideon, his family, and the nation. How did this happen? How did something that started so well turn out like this? Is there a particular event we can point to as a turning point? There just might be. To understand this, we need to get back to the real story at the point we typically quit telling it.

Though the Midianite army was routed and fleeing, Gideon was not content with that. Taking his tired and unprovisioned 300 with him, he crossed the Jordan in pursuit (8:4). He approached the cities of Succoth and Penuel to diplomatically demand they provision his band of soldiers. Both cities refused, and he warned them they would face dire consequences upon his return (8:5-9). With the Midianite remnant feeling safe on the east side of the Jordan, Gideon was able to sneak up on them and route them again (8:11-12). He captured the two remaining kings and explained that he was killing them to avenge family members who had died at the hands of the Midianite army (8:18-19). When he was unsuccessful in forcing his son to execute the kings, Gideon did it himself (8:20-21). Prior to this, he revisited the towns he had threatened and carried out the threats. He had the leadership of Succoth beaten, and killed the men of Penuel (8:14-17).

There is nothing simple about this story. When did things begin to go badly? The text, at the very least, hints that it was when he crossed the river. Throughout the story, to this point, he had relied on the Lord every step of the way. He worked to be sure that he had God's approval and that God was with him. (To see just one example of this, read 6:36-40.) Now Gideon seems to be crossing the river without God. He had taken it upon himself to enlist the aid of additional soldiers under his command prior to crossing the river despite the entire rationale for the very limited number of men God provided for him (7:23-25). On the east side of the Jordan, there is no indication that he is acting on God's directions or that he had factored God into his plans. The only times he mentions God seem to be in a self-serving, manipulative way. He appears to be driven by an angry desire to avenge his family.

Sidebar

With the mistakes he made, how did Gideon "make the list" of people of faith in Hebrews 11:32-33? It was "by faith" that he conquered the Midianites—at least in the initial battle that God sanctioned. "Making the list" did not mean that you were not someone who struggled and made mistakes. He is listed with Samson, David, and Jephthah as well as other imperfect people. There is no doubt that in spite of his failings, Gideon did good things for the people (Judges 8:35).

His dealing with Succoth and Penuel is the most difficult to assess. Perhaps they failed to provide the assistance they should have provided. Maybe they received the punishment they deserved, and Gideon's actions were justified. However, and I would suggest more likely, there is a different and better explanation. Maybe he was acting without God's mandate, so they owed him nothing. Therefore, he had no right to politely or otherwise demand they provision his soldiers. He had no right to kill his brethren for failing to meet his demands. However we assess this, it is clear that he experienced a dramatic change during the story. He went from being someone who was unsure of himself, humble, and constantly inquiring of and seeking assurances from God to someone who was self-confident, bold, assertive, demanding, and aggressive. He went from someone who destroyed an altar dedicated to an idol to someone who constructed something that he and his family worshiped as an idol. The idolatry that he was responsible for was perhaps even more dangerous than the worship of Canaanite gods or the gods of their oppressors. The worship of foreign gods was obviously something that came from the outside and could be opposed from that standpoint. It was worshiping gods other than the God of Israel. This homegrown variety blended acknowledging the true God with pagan practices. It associated the great victory given by God with a graven image. Gideon creating an idol surely contributed greatly to the people going all the way to the worship of Baal after he died and even worshiping one named "Baal of the covenant" (Baal-berith, 8:33).

Lessons

As will be true with every character we study, Gideon reminds us that our all-powerful God can and does take imperfect people and enlists and empowers them to do some amazing things. That gives even me hope.

The world around us is a dangerous place. We know it, so we must be careful and alert. Sadly, "out there" is not the only place danger exists and threatens us. Sometimes it comes from nearby. Like Gideon and the ephod, it may be from someone close to us who we respect and love. When that is the case, as sad as it sometimes is, it can be even more dangerous than error from the outside. It is harder to recognize, and we may cross the line between giving people the benefit of the doubt and closing our eyes to their mistakes or making excuses for them. We must be alert to dangers from without and within.

Anger combined with a desire for vengeance can be a terribly destructive combination. If we allow it to, it will drive us to the point our judgment is clouded, we lose our concern for others, our motives are corrupted, and we undo good we may have otherwise done.

Success is great, but it can lead to a variety of problems. It may cause us to become proud. When we act out that pride it may show itself in a variety of ways. We may treat others badly because we feel superior to them. Or, we may ignore the rules because we feel they don't apply to us. We may even take credit for something we do not deserve. As Proverbs reminds us, pride leads to destruction.

One reason God hates lying is because it causes people to act out of a false sense of reality. When we cause others to do that, we have harmed them. Perhaps the most dangerous person we can do that to is ourselves. When we, either before or after the fact, begin the process of rationalizing and justifying our bad behavior, we may convince ourselves that our evil is actually good. When we find ourselves doing bad things and feel justified, there is nothing to cause us to reflect and repent. That's a really bad place to be.

Our choices often have consequences that we had not intended. Sometimes, if it's a good choice, these unintended consequences turn out to be great blessings. Other times, not so much. We cannot predict with certainty what we may set in motion with what we do, but it's important to think about what might happen. If our choice is a good one in itself, we can't feel pressured to forgo it simply because something bad might possibly happen down the road. On the other hand, if it's a marginal or unnecessary decision that can lead to obvious problems, why do it?

Questions

1. What was Gideon doing when the angel appeared to him? How would you characterize his demeanor during the meeting?

2. Why did he destroy the altar of Baal at night?

3. Describe his seeking of assurance in 6:36-40.

4. What was the process God used to limit his band of fighters to 300?

5. What finally gave Gideon the courage he needed to begin the battle? (7:13-15)

6. 7:22 attributes their victory to God, while 8:11-12 does not. What might explain the difference?

7. How does 8:35 summarize his contribution to the people?

Discussion

1. Some have argued that we see a very early indication that Gideon's attitude was changing for the worse as early as 7:20. Do you see anything there that might suggest that?

2. Gideon seems to have said "no" but done "yes" to the offer of being king. Do we ever say "no" but do "yes?" How might we do that?

3. Is it conceivable that Gideon imagined a legitimate use for the ephod? What might that have been? How could it have morphed into an idol?

4. Can you see any circumstances in the story where Gideon may not have been honest with himself? Why is that such a dangerous type of dishonesty?

5. I do not believe that Gideon intended to do anything that would lead the people into idolatry. Do we ever make choices that have repercussions far beyond what we had imagined? Can you cite some examples of how that could happen?

Samson

His story is "well-known" and much loved. He was the guy with bulging muscles who continually attacked the Philistines until his evil wife tricked him into revealing the secret of his strength so she could take it away from him. When his hair and strength returned, he killed many more Philistines and destroyed their pagan temple. Does that sound about right?

What do you remember about the story? What lessons have you learned from it?

The synopsis I provided sadly provides a fairly typical cherry-picked, sanitized version of the story many of us learned. The problem is the true story that God wanted us to know is much more complex than that. To help us accomplish this:

- Look at the story more carefully.
- Identify certain character traits of Samson that are emphasized in the text.
- See what lessons we need to learn from his life.

Circumstances

The Philistines were another, and particularly nasty, example of surrounding nations that oppressed Israel. As Judges 13 opens, they have been doing this for 40 years. Once again God would raise up a deliverer. This chosen one would be born to a barren woman and her husband. The angel of the Lord appeared to them to announce this good news (Jud. 13:2-4). For people who know some of the Bible stories, this is a really exciting combination. Some of the greatest heroes of the Bible were born to barren women and were announced by angels. When we combine this with the special instructions for the way the child was to live his life, as well as how his mother was to conduct herself during the pregnancy, we have great expectations for this person (Jud. 13:4-5). The response of his parents was also impressive. They wanted to be sure they understood exactly what they were to do in rearing the child and preparing him for his mission (Jud. 13:8,12). As promised, she conceived and gave birth to Samson who grew and was blessed by the Lord. It is a bit odd that she named him "Samson," which probably means something like "little sun," rather than a name containing a reference to God. This probably reflects the general pagan influence in the land as well as some lack of spiritual perceptiveness on her part.

Samson Gets Married

Chapters 14 and 15 contain a series of interesting parallels in describing the heart of his time as a judge. Samson was very much an impulsive and senses-driven person, and this typically gets him into trouble. We see this throughout the story, beginning in 14:1. He saw a Philistine girl he was attracted to, so he demanded that his parents arrange for them to be married. He saw her and said that she was right in his eyes. He wanted the arrangements to be made immediately. Despite his parents' misgivings, they gave in to this demand.

Note: verse 4 should not be seen as God causing or even approving his choice to marry an inhabitant of the land, but as an example of God using Samson's desire to accomplish his own purpose. (As an example of this, see Gen. 50:20.) Verse 4 tells us that God sought an occasion, but not that he motivated Samson's actions or approved of his choices.

While traveling to Timnah during the process of arranging the marriage, a young lion attacked him. This story of Samson killing the lion with his bare hands shows both his physical strength as well as his disregard for the Law. As a Nazarite, he was forbidden to touch a dead body. There were provisions made for an occurrence such as this, but he chose to ignore them (Num. 6:9-12). While touching it in the process of killing the animal was understandable, his later choice to touch it to extract honey was inexcusable (Jud. 14:8-9). The odd circumstances of a hive in a lion carcass provided him with a riddle he used to try to win a fortune in clothes from his new wife's family. Unable to solve the riddle, the Philistines threatened to burn down her family's house if she couldn't give them the answer (Jud 14:15). After enduring seven days of her pleading and cajoling, he relented and gave her the answer in time to ensure that he lost the wager. In his rage, the Lord gave him the physical strength he needed to kill 30 Philistines to take their clothes to pay his debt (Jud. 14:18-20). This was not an act of war on the enemies of the people. Given his motives, it was murder and theft. Rather than going back to his wife, he went home. During the interim, his father-in-law assumed he was abandoning her, so he gave her to another man.

Ongoing Conflict

At this point, Samson determines to do great harm to the Philistines. The wording of verse 3 is difficult, but it at least raises the possibility that while he might recognize some of his previous behavior was not justified, what he was about to do was. Regardless, once again his creativity was on display. He utilized 300 foxes (or jackals) to burn up the Philistines' crops and orchards (Jud. 15:5). The Philistines responded to this economic disaster by killing his wife and father-in-law. This escalation resulted in Samson vowing revenge (Jud. 15:7), followed with the rather odd promise to stop at that point. Once again, he is demonstrating that he has little under-standing of his mission or what God is accomplishing through him.

The men of Judah had accepted Philistine domination and feared upsetting the status quo (Jud. 15:11). The duplicity of the tribe of Judah provided the opportunity for Samson to kill 1000 Philistines (Jud. 15:15). His weapon of choice was a bone from an unclean animal, and his contact with the bone once again violated his Nazarite vow.

No doubt killing 1,000 men with a jawbone would be tiring and leave one thirsty. His concern for his own welfare leads him to do something we have no record of him having done before. That was to call out to God and at least to some degree acknowledge his role in the victory (Jud. 15:18). While there is something positive in this, it once again calls attention to his senses-driven selfishness. God providing the water was an expression of grace, and not proof that he approved of Samson. (See Num. 20:2-13.)

The limits of his success as a judge seem to be emphasized as chapter 15 ends with a statement about his time that fails to state, as is typically the case, that the "land had rest," and shows the enemy to still be in at least partial control during that time. 15:20 may set the stage for the final acts of his career. As chapter 16 be-gins, we find him traveling the length of Philistia. It looks like a premeditated decision to go to an evil city to misbehave. The story of him "eyeing" a Philistine prostitute that he has sex with sets the stage for another example of his sensual behavior providing an opportunity for the power of God to display itself as he rendered the city less easily defended by tearing down and carrying away the doors of the gate of the city (Jud. 16:3).

A Tragic Ending

The final, and perhaps best-known event in his story began with him being attracted to another Philistine woman named Delilah.

Her name means "night." "Little sun" was meeting "darkness" (Jud. 16:4). The Philistines know Samson's penchant for their women well enough to know that this is the way to get him to reveal the source of his strength. Apparently, as soon as they began their relationship, she allowed herself to be bribed by the Philistines to learn his source of strength. The previous incident of him destroying the city gate provided powerful incentive for them to destroy him. With 1,100 pieces of silver from each of the five Philistine cities, the price she was paid is mind-boggling. Though it was clear that she was trying to get the secret of his strength to betray him, he stayed with her and finally gave up the secret (Jud. 16:17). It's also ironic that he reveals his deepest secret to a pagan woman who isn't even his wife.

Sidebar: Samson's Strength

Having long hair did not make Samson strong. The strength was provided by the Lord, but that provision was predicated on Samson following God's instructions to not cut his hair. It is quite possible that his physique was not incredibly impressive. Had he been a huge person with bulging muscles, the source of his strength would have appeared to be less of a mystery.

When his hair was cut as he slept, his strength did leave him, and the Philistines were able to take him prisoner. The wording that describes this is tragic. Verse 20 says that the Lord had left him. Perhaps God's long-suffering dealing with him was finally exhausted when he broke the final part of his Nazarite vow. The weakened Samson had his eyes gouged out, and he was put to the most menial, difficult, and humiliating task imaginable. While he had joked about making the Philistines beasts of burden, he had become that, and his eyes that had gotten him into so much trouble were taken from him.

To celebrate what they perceived to be the victory of their god Dagon over Samson and his God, the Philistine elite gathered in the

Temple of Dagon to celebrate. During the period of his servitude, his hair had grown again (Jud. 16:22). When he called on the Lord to give him strength one more time, the Lord listened and gave him the power to bring down the Philistine-filled building and kill the 3,000 inside. Samson died with them (Jud. 16:30). The tragedy of his personal failures and unrealized potential are captured in the statement of verses 28 and 30. Though he did call on the Lord to ask for the ability to destroy the temple, his motive was personal revenge, and he accomplished more by dying that he had by living. Thus, a story that began with a barren woman having a child ended with a wounded warrior bringing death.

His story is not a pretty one and, were it not for the statement in Hebrew 11:32, we might dismiss him as nothing more than a bad guy that God used to accomplish his own purposes. It is good to note that he is included in the list in Hebrews 11, which mentions others who were surely imperfect men given to, at least on occasion, impulsive behavior and following their lust. We must not allow our assumptions of the text in Hebrews to cause us to ignore the facts about his failings stated in Judges. Though Samson's example is extreme, he did not forget the Lord, and called out to him, realizing that God was the source of his strength. This may explain why, despite his failings, he is listed as an example of someone who by faith helped defeat the enemies of God's people. Samson had many advantages and gifts. He was strong, creative, and despite his bent towards brutish behavior, probably had a good deal of intelligence. He threw this away and became another example of wasted potential. As a deliverer, he was both the strongest and the weakest.

Before we find ourselves feeling sorry for the nation, we should realize that unlike other occasions, they had not appealed to God for deliverance. They seemed to be apathetic about the whole thing. Judah, which should have been a leading tribe, represented contentment with pagan domination. As far as a deliverer, the nation got what it deserved.

Lessons

This story is, first and foremost, a story about how God can and will use the choices that people make to accomplish his purposes. It is important to understand that being utilized by God is not the same as being approved by God.

Samson continually displayed a disregard for authority. This disrespect seems to have begun with disregard for his parents, but it also reflected itself in his disrespect for God. Disrespect for legitimate authority will manifest itself in multiple relationships, likely including our relationship with God.

It also shows us that the influence of a good family does not ensure good behavior on the part of the child. While being presented as basically good people, the story also seems to present his parents as being too indulgent. Perhaps their joy in having a child, especially one that was chosen for great things caused them to "spoil" him.

His life demonstrated, again and again, the dangers of being impulsive, lacking self-control, and being driven by his physical desires. It was also a reminder that being "right" about some things doesn't excuse bad behavior in other areas.

Personal revenge should never drive our behavior. Chapters 14 and 15 demonstrate how seeking revenge causes an insatiable cycle when both parties seek it. It's a shame that his acts of war against the enemy of the people of God were not motivated by a desire to protect the nation or vindicate the name of God. The attitude that David displayed in reacting to Goliath is a much better model (1 Sam. 17:26,36).

Questions

1. List some examples of barren women in the Bible enabled by God to have a child. Which of these births were announced by angels?

2. At the end of Judges 13, did everything seem to be in place for Samson to be a great man and spiritual leader?

3. What assurance did he demand from the men of Judah before allowing himself to be bound? Why did he do this? Describe the loosing of the rope.

4. Describe the sequence of efforts made by Delilah to find out the source of his strength. Why did he keep going along with her efforts? Do you think he really believed anything could take his strength?

5. On what other occasion did the Philistines use a woman to get a secret from Samson?

6. List the conflicts that Samson had with the Philistines. What impact would each have had on them? What motivated him on each occasion?

Discussion

1. Can having great expectations for a child sometimes lead parents to be too indulgent? Can you see an example of this in Samson's family?

2. Does it seem at least a little ironic that Samson was brought down by a materialistic person?

3. Can you think of some evil people in the Bible who were utilized by God to accomplish his purposes?

4. Discuss the complexity of Samson's character displayed in Judges 16:28.

5. How might we fall into the trap of thinking that because we are "right" about "the big things" that other things in our lives really don't matter?

Elijah

Elijah was surely a hero by any metrics. From the whirlwind to Heaven to making an appearance at the transfiguration of Jesus to being cited as an example of the power of prayer, he is mentioned more than 100 times in the Bible in a dozen different books. Given so much data, we tend to look at specific incidents rather than his whole life. In this study, we will begin with a brief overview and then dig a little deeper into some of the complexities he faced. As always, we will conclude by thinking about some lessons we can learn from the challenges he faced.

The Story We Know

We probably remember some of the exciting, dramatic, miraculous stories from his life like:

- God's miraculous provisions for him
- Raising a dead boy
- A confrontation with a wicked king and pagan prophets
- A contest to show who is truly God
- A conversation that included amazing forces of nature
- The whirlwind and fiery chariots

Let's do a synopsis as a reminder.

Our story begins with him bursting onto the scene in 1 Kings 17 to announce a three-year drought as punishment for the wickedness of the nation. During this time, God miraculously provided for his needs, first as ravens brought him what would have been sumptuous fare as he lived near a stream (17:6), and then through a widow in Sidon (17:16). Going into this heartland of Baal worship and being provided for by the least likely of people during a time when the false storm god Baal was being shown to be ineffectual in providing for his own territory was a powerful testimony about the one true God. When the widow's son became ill and died, Elijah was able to raise him from the dead (17:22).

A Great Victory

As the time for the drought to end drew near, Elijah began his trek to confront King Ahab and the false prophets. It began with a meeting with a courageous court official named Obadiah who was responsible for hiding and feeding 100 true prophets (18:4). Despite being under a death-threat, he confronted the angry king (18:16), and called for a contest with the prophets supported by the throne and representing the false gods (18:19). When, after an extended period of time that saw the prophets of Baal vainly and frantically calling on Baal to send fire to consume their offering, Elijah mocked their futile efforts. He then constructed an alter that represented the 12 tribes, and prepared the sacrifice which he doused it with water. In response to him calling on God, fire came from Heaven that consumed altar and all. Elijah then called upon the people to kill the false prophets. They responded by both confessing their sins and killing the prophets of Baal (18:38-39). With rain then on the way, Elijah's successful day was capped by outrunning the royal chariot back to the capitol.

What an absolutely incredible and successful day. Baal had been exposed, the false prophets eliminated, and the people repented. Elijah was on top of the world!

But—the story isn't over.

- It gets more complex.
- It has actually been more complex the whole time.

To this point, Elijah doesn't remind me of me at all (James 5:17). It appears that he has marched courageously and confidently from one difficult situation to another without any doubts, fears, or setbacks, and with a future that looks bright. That isn't the case at all. Doubts and fears that he had surely been facing all along (See the story of the death of the widow's son in more detail) now erupt with a vengeance as an evil queen, Jezebel, vows vengeance on him (1 Kings 19:2). Suddenly, in fear, he is running for his life to the other end of the land where he stops and asks God if he can die (I Kings 19:3-4).

A couple of quick points:

- With God's protection, he wasn't really in danger.
- If he really wanted to die, why not save the long trip south?

God's response was to send and angel to strengthen him for an additional trip and 40 day fast ((I Kings 19:8). Upon arriving at the mountain of God and while hiding in a cave, a conversation ensues. God begins by asking him what he was doing there (9). It was a question not asked for information, but to cause Elijah to stop and reflect on what he was feeling and why. His response was to tell God he was the last faithful person left. In response, God sent a great wind, an earthquake, a fire, and a low whisper (I Kings 19:11). The text tells us that God was not "in" any of the first three, and it does not tell us if he was "in" the last. It may be that he was in the low whisper and that was to teach Elijah that sometimes God is in the simple and quiet things rather than in obvious and powerful manifestations. Or, it may be that it was only after the first three subsided and he thought the coast was clear that Elijah finally came out of hiding and continued the conversation (I Kings 19:13).

When the conversation continued, God told him to get up and get busy (I Kings 19:15-17). He had three jobs for him to do. It was only in a very veiled way that he connected these tasks to Elijah's fears or the evil of Ahab and Jezebel. Then, after telling him to get busy, he adds as almost an afterthought that there are actually still 7,000who are still faithful to him (I Kings 19:18).

Elijah did these jobs, and the impact for good was profound. The result was the end of the house of Ahab, breaking Phoenician influence in the land, and destroying Baal worship in Israel. Finally, after this, he was taken to Heaven in a whirlwind (2 Kings 2:11).

Lessons
The applications for our lives in this story abound, so let's focus on a few.

It's important for us to see, appreciate, and be encouraged by the "small victories." It seems like Elijah was failing to do this during the time he felt like a failure, when he was alone and wanted to die. The reality was he had seen many good and encouraging things to build him up and provide hope during difficult times. When we only look at huge "wins" and what is happening right now, we set ourselves up for periods of discouragement. We work for great things, but as we do, we need to see the "small" blessings and encouraging things around us.

Loneliness is a huge problem in our society for people of all ages. Elijah struggled with that. Feeling lonely does not mean that you are alone. As God was always with Elijah, he is with us as well. Not only was God with Elijah, but there were other people of God with him. We need to recognize this and seek their companionship.

God's message to Elijah during the time Elijah was feeling so discouraged was not something that pampered him and fed into his struggle with self-pity. He doesn't say, "Oh Elijah, you are so wonderful, and I appreciate you so much. Just relax and watch while I take care of everything, and then you will feel better." The message was to get up and get busy. Often the best medicine for us when we are feeling down, discouraged, and sorry for ourselves is to look to the needs of others and the work God has for us to do.

Elijah would not have understood how the tasks God gave him would ultimately work out in accomplishing good, but he needed to do them, trusting that God knew what needed to be done and his purposes would be accomplished. We need the same kind of faith. We need to be busy doing what God tells us to do while trusting that it is valuable and does matter even when we don't understand why, how, or see the results.

Finally, we need to trust that God will not have expectations of us that exceed what he will empower us to do. With that assurance, let's be busy in his service, relying on his strength, following his instructions, and trusting in his wisdom.

Questions

1. How did God provide for Elijah, the widow, and her son (1 Kings 17:-16)?

2. Who was Obadiah, and how did he fit into the story (1 Kings 18:3-16)?

3. How many false prophets did Elijah confront (1 Kings 18:19)?

4. Why was Elijah so frightened of Jezebel (1 Kings 19:1-3)?

5. Describe in your own words how Elijah was taken to Heaven (2 Kings 2:1-11).

Discussion

1. What were some of the "small victories" Elijah had seen/experienced that the Bible text calls attention to? What kinds of small victories can we find in our lives?

2. Do you ever feel alone? What helps you to remember that you are not? What can we do to remind ourselves that God is near and to feel his presence? How can you reach out to others who are lonely? How will this help both of you?

3. What are some things you realize God expects you to do that you can't see immediate results from?

4. What are some of the ways that you can relate to Elijah now more than you could before this lesson?

Uzziah

Who? Was he the guy that touched the ark and died? Maybe he was the husband of Bathsheba that David had killed… No, and though we may have never heard of him, he was one of the most significant kings of Judah, and his story is quite complex. Since most are probably not familiar with him at all, we need to start with a little background before we even get into his story.

Context

Let's start with his father, King Amaziah. Amaziah, on balance, was not a bad king, but he was not one of the most faithful either (2 Kings 14:3). He obeyed the Law in some things (2 Kings 14:4-6), but he failed to tear down the places where the people worshiped false gods (2 Kings 14:4). He went to war with the Edomites and won a great victory, but this victory was tainted by his errors. First, he unwisely hired mercenaries from Israel to help. When the prophet of God instructed him to fire the mercenaries, he did, but they proceeded to raid, loot, and kill the people of Judah on their way home (2 Chron. 25:9-13). After Amaziah defeated the Edomites, he decided to take their idols home and worship them (2 Chron. 25:14-16).

He decided to worship the gods of a people he had defeated rather than the God who gave him victory.

Filled with pride after his victory, Amaziah decided to go to war against Israel. Joash, king of Israel, defeated Amaziah, tore down some of the walls of Jerusalem, took hostages, and looted the Temple (2 Chron. 25:23-24). His enemies in Jerusalem conspired to kill him, and they managed to do so when they found him in Lachish. When he was killed, the people chose to put his 16-year-old son Uzziah on the throne (2 Chron. 26:1).

Uzziah (2 Kings uses a different form of his name—Azariah) inherited some complex circumstances from his father. The people were openly practicing idolatry, they had been humiliated by Israel, and hundreds of feet of the city walls had been torn down. No doubt these were difficult times for a young man to become king.

Great Start

He began his reign in the best possible way as he "set himself to seek God" (2 Chron. 26:5). This included him listening to the wise instructions of a prophet named Zechariah. (This is not the Zechariah who wrote the book that bears this name.) As long as he followed this path, things were wonderful. Overall, his reign represented some of the brightest days for Judah. He was an intelligent and creative leader who cared about God and the people he ruled. As a military leader, his success would remind people of the great days of David, and he was the greatest builder since Solomon.

It was, perhaps, the humiliating capture of Jerusalem that caused him to strengthen the cities defense. (Part of his work might also have been repairing damage done by a powerful earthquake that occurred during his reign [Amos 1:1, Zech. 14:5].) In addition to repairing the damage to the walls Joash had done, he added additional fortifications (2 Chron. 26:9). He also utilized special equipment his engineers had invented to help protect the city (2 Chron. 26:15). His army was very large, well organized, and equipped. He had a group of men that either represented a professional core of officers or elite special forces. Unlike the earlier conscript army, weapons were provided from the royal armory (2 Chron. 26:12-14).

Sidebar: Uzziah's War Machines

It isn't clear what type of equipment this was. Some translations lead us to the idea that these machines were some sort of torsion-based apparatuses like a primitive catapult. This may be accurate, but there is no other record of similar things from that time period. The detailed Lachish reliefs do not depict something like this. They do, however, show some special frames on the walls that allowed the defenders to more effectively use their weapons. Perhaps this is what was meant.

He did not use his military might simply for defense, and when he went on the attack, he had the good of the nation in mind. He successfully expanded their borders to the south and west to their greatest limits since the days of Solomon. He fought against the Philistines, Ammonites, and Arabs (2 Chron. 26:6-8). These victories were not only for territorial expansion back into the promised borders, but were great for trade. The Philistines had been a thorn in Israel's side for centuries, and by taking the territory he did, it gave Judah control of a major trade route, the Coastal Highway. Eloth (Elat) was a port on the Red Sea that Solomon had conquered and used for trade with Arabia, Africa, and India. The Edomites had taken it, but Uzziah took it back to reestablish that valuable avenue for trade.

Uzziah the Great Builder

"He built towers in the wilderness and hewed many cisterns, for he had much livestock, both in the lowland and in the plain. He also had plowmen and vinedressers in the hill country and the fertile fields, for he loved the soil" (2 Chron. 26:10, NASV).

Archeologists have found remains of projects from this period in several places. The towers he built provided protection as well as possibly offering shelter for workers and storage areas. His cisterns allowed for an adequate and stable source of fresh water. He was also heavily involved in agriculture. His focus on infrastructure and economic prosperity in addition to his military prowess resulted in him being famous for his strength and success throughout the region.

"The Ammonites also gave tribute to Uzziah, and his fame extended to the border of Egypt, for he became very strong" (2 Chron. 26:8, NASV).

It's a great story! What is there not to love about it? He came into a less than great situation and did an amazing job of turning things around. But it is a more complex story than we have seen so far.

Tragic Turn
His tremendous success and acclaim created the opportunity for his fall. It resulted in a degree of pride so strong that, "he acted corruptly, and he was unfaithful to the LORD his God" (2 Chron. 26:16).

He entered the Temple in an attempt to burn incense on the Altar of Incense. Only the descendants of Aaron were permitted to do this (Ex. 30:1-10). This type of presumptuous behavior was not new. This type of usurping authority went back at least as far as the days of Miriam and Korah (Num. 12:10, 16:1), and was the downfall of two previous kings. Because Saul offered a sacrifice, he was told that his kingdom would end (1 Sam. 13:9,14). In the story of Jeroboam's apostasy, his offering incense seems to have been the climactic moment leading to his condemnation (1 Kings 12:33-13:1). With him on the very brink of this offense, Azariah and 80 other priests confronted him to stop him from offering the sacrifice. They challenged him from God's word and warned him of the consequences of his actions (2 Chron. 26:18). We need to be impressed with the faithfulness of the priests and the courage they displayed. Uzziah's grandfather Joash had killed the priest of God for confronting him (2 Chron. 24:22).

Sadly, rather than realizing his error, Uzziah was filled with anger. We don't know what expression of rage might have been in his heart, because at that moment God intervened and struck him with a terrible skin disease. Only then did he flee the Temple (2 Chron. 26:19-20). This disease that stayed with him for the rest of his life not only caused great suffering, but it also left him ritually unclean. This uncleanness left him unable to carry out his role as king and meant he had to live in isolation for the rest of his days (Lev. 13:46). Even in death he was separated from the kings who had come before him, and his legacy was as a "leper" (2 Chron. 26:23). Thus tragically ended his 52 year reign.

Lessons

1. His great successes as a king were clearly connected to the fact that he sought God and listened to the man of God who advised him. That's how it works. The best, happiest, and most productive lives we can live under our circumstances are lives when we seek God and allow his words to direct us.

2. It is interesting to note that the text evaluates his reign in this way: "He did right in the sight of the LORD, according to all that his father Amaziah had done" (2 Kings 15:3, NASV).

   On balance, he, like his father, was, for the most part, good. It is important to remember that he overcame many of the challenges and did not repeat some of the mistakes of his father. That is often very difficult to do. There is no indication that he participated in idolatry. In fact, his sin was related to the worship of the true God in the Temple. Also, he must have sustained a wise relationship with the kings of Israel, especially Jeroboam II. He is to be commended for overcoming the negative influence of his father.

3. Sadly, his father's influence was not the only influence he overcame. "He continued to seek God in the days of Zechariah, who had understanding through the vision of God; and as long as he sought the LORD, God prospered him" (2 Chron. 26:5, NASV).

The clear implication of the text is that as long as Zechariah was alive, Uzziah allowed him to provide a good influence for him. When this godly advisor was gone, so was the good influence. It may well be that the change that took place in his character corresponded to the loss of that respected voice. Many of us have had those who were powerful influences for good in our lives. Perhaps they provided continual feedback on our choices and we feared disappointing them. That's wonderful, but it is not enough. We must come to the point that principles of faith are so internalized and ingrained in us that we continue to do what's right even after our spiritual mentors are gone.

4. Though he overcame much of the legacy of his father, he had one glaring and tragic similarity: pride. We sometimes say that an athlete becomes overconfident because he begins to believe all of the good things his admirers say about him. That may have been the case with Uzziah when he became famous and powerful. Pride not only enthrones us in a place we don't belong, but it dethrones God at the same time. When Uzziah began to see himself as more than he was, he was seeing God as less than he is. When he decided to ignore what God said about offering the sacrifice, he was claiming greater authority than God. That was compounded by his response to God's messenger. Pride also leads to other sins. It led to an unrighteous anger directed at the courageous priests. That type of anger often leads to even more bad choices. The Book of Proverbs was likely used as a textbook for young nobles preparing for a life of service. The compiler would have realized that privileged position, talent, and success would often lead to pride. Surely Uzziah had heard the words that pride leads to destruction (Prov. 16:18) but imagined that would never be true of him. His reality was that when he sought an honor that was not his, he lost the honor he had. When he tried to function in an office that

wasn't his, he lost the office he had. His pride led to him losing his sole reign as king, being excluded from worship, being banished from his palace, being quarantined from people, and not being buried with his ancestors. Pride will take us down the same road.

5. When he lost his willingness to listen, he was doomed. The Book of Proverbs repeatedly speaks of listening as a source of wisdom and as a manifestation of it as well. Those instructions will sometimes come in the form of being "called out" for our mistakes (See Prov. 1:5, 19:20, 12:15, 15:31). We don't like being told we are wrong, and may not even like having anyone tell us what to do, but if we are unwilling to listen we will not be able to grow, improve, or make corrections in our lives.

6. Finally, his example brings to mind a couple of additional aspects of sin. A moment of sin can and often will overshadow much good in our lives. Consequences that we suffer will often last the rest of our lives. He could have been remembered as one of the greatest kings in the Bible, but in addition to the other consequences we have discussed, he is more famous for his disease and being the guy who was ruling when the big earthquake hit. Also, sin leads to exclusion. He was excluded from worship and from God's people. Sin in our lives will ultimately lead us to being excluded from God's presence forever.

Questions

1. What good things and what bad things do you think Uzziah may have learned from his father?

2. Explain the expression "set himself to seek God." How does one do that?

3. Locate the sites of his conquest on a map. Consider the strategic value of these locations.

4. What is a cistern, and how does it work?

5. How close was Uzziah to offering the sacrifice?

6. Describe the courage displayed by the priests.

Discussion

1. Because of his father's rule, what are some of the pressures Uzziah might have faced as he began to reign?

2. What are some things that make it difficult to overcome the negative in our environment?

3. Is there a spiritual mentor in your life who helps keep you close to God? How are you preparing yourself for a time when that person is not around?

4. When we have success, do we sometimes forget that it comes from God? How can we protect ourselves from pride?

5. How can we become better listeners? How do we feel when we are corrected by someone?

6. Imagine how terrible it was for Uzziah to be excluded from worship and God's people. How terrible would it be to be excluded from those things forever?

Manasseh

If you have ever heard of him, it was almost surely in a totally negative light. You may remember him from the list of wicked kings of Judah, but nothing else about him. Truly he did a lot of horrible things and caused a great deal of harm. In fact, 2 Kings 21:12 attributes the destruction of Judah to him. As bad as he was, it's not that simple. It is rather more complex.

Since we don't know his story well at all, we need to begin with a little background. We will follow that with looking at his story—including the shocking ending. Of course, we will finish by looking at some lessons for us today.

Context

His father was Hezekiah, one of the greatest kings of Judah. He worked to rid the land of idolatry and restore true worship. However, the Assyrians had managed to conquer much of Judah. Hezekiah had become ill and was told he would die. After praying to God, his life was extended by 15 years (2 Kings 20:6). During part of this time, he reigned as coregent with his son Manasseh. This began when Manasseh was only 12 years old and lasted for 10 years. Since Hezekiah knew how long he had to live, he likely wanted to spend time training his son to rule.

Manasseh, King of Judah

From reading the description of his reign, one might wonder if he had read the Law in order to be sure he violated every part of it. The things he was responsible for read like a laundry list of the things forbidden by Moses. 2 Kings 21:2-7,16 provide a list of the idolatrous practices he was responsible for committing. He was also a vassal of the Assyrians with his name appearing in two different Assyrian texts. The relationship with the Assyrians and reinstitution of idolatry were probably connected.

Most of the idolatry mentioned in the text was of Canaanite origin and had been disrupted by Hezekiah. The people may have mistakenly connected their servility to the Assyrians with their repudiation of Canaanite gods. Perhaps Manasseh was guilty of the same error or simply gave in to popular demand. Either way, there must have been those who opposed going back into idolatry. One of the sins he was guilty of was shedding "very much innocent blood, till he had filled Jerusalem from one end to another" (2 Kings 21:16). Those slain probably included those from among the prophets and priests who opposed his wickedness. (According to a reference in the Talmud, he even had Isaiah killed.) Also, while the Assyrians did not force their gods on land not incorporated into Assyria, there can be little doubt they exerted an influence on the religious practices of vassal people. Two practices, in particular, demonstrate the incredible depth to which he sank into egregious pagan worship. According to 2 Kings 21:4, he built pagan altars in the Temple. Perhaps even more shocking, he burned his own son as a sacrifice (2 Kings 21:6). It is not surprising that his deeds are described as they are in 2 Chron 33:9: "Manasseh led Judah and the inhabitants of Jerusalem astray, to do more evil than the nations whom the LORD destroyed before the people of Israel."

God called on the people to repent, but they refused. In another effort to bring them back, God sent the Assyrian army to capture Manasseh. The particulars of this are uncertain, but perhaps Manasseh joined an unsuccessful rebellion against the Assyrian king. On at least two other occasions, vassal kings who had rebelled or were suspected of disloyalty were captured and held for a period to ensure their loyalty.

Sidebar

2 Kings does not include the account of Manasseh being taken to Babylon or of his repentance. That should not cast doubt on the historical accuracy of the story. On the other hand, given the emphasis on covenantal faithfulness and restoration in 2 Chronicles, it is to be expected that a story like this would be included there.

The process of taking Manasseh to Babylon was designed to be extremely humiliating. It involved the use of not only shackles, but also hooks likely attached to his body (2 Chron 33:11). Assyrian reliefs show captives being treated this way. God's dramatic actions to bring him to repentance succeeded.

An Amazing Change

"And when he was in distress, he entreated the favor of the LORD his God and humbled himself greatly before the God of his fathers. He prayed to him, and God was moved by his entreaty and heard his plea and brought him again to Jerusalem into his kingdom. Then Manasseh knew that the LORD was God" (2 Chron. 33:12-13, ESV).

Side bar

There is a 15-verse text that appears in the Bibles used by Eastern Orthodox and Assyrian Churches called the Prayer of Manasseh. It was also included in the Vulgate as well as a couple early English translations. However, it was clearly not composed by Manasseh. It dates to the very late Second Temple Period. And while it does not contain any reference to Manasseh, it may have been inspired by his story. It was nicely written, but theologically flawed. It claims that Abraham, Isaac, and Jacob never sinned.

After Solomon had dedicated the Temple, God spoke to him and told him what would be necessary for the people to do if they would be forgiven and blessed (2 Chron. 7:14). What the text tells us that Manasseh did fit this perfectly. His circumstances humbled him and caused him to look to God for help. His genuinely penitent heart caused God to listen and allow him to go home.

His conduct upon returning to Jerusalem showed that he truly had changed. We cannot say for sure what political factors led him to do the building projects described in 2 Chronicles 33:14. Perhaps it was with the approval of the Assyrians to help Jerusalem protect the Assyrian frontier, or maybe it was a gesture of independence reflecting a determination to rely on God for protection. Either way, increasing army size and building projects are marks of righteous kings in the Chronicles. God was indeed blessing him.

He also did what he could to reverse the idolatry in the land and restore true worship. The text tells us that he tore down the altars to false gods he had built, including those in the Temple. He also restored true worship (2 Chron. 33:15-16). In many ways, the story has a happy ending, but it is more complex than that.

Damage Done

Though his reforms had a positive impact, it was limited and temporary. The worship of the people was not completely reformed even in his lifetime. Though not worshiping false gods, the people continued to worship at the pagan cultic sites (2 Chron. 33:17). His son, Amon, reverted to the previous idolatry. The text specifically connects his evil to what his father had done (2 Chron. 33:22). During the two years Amon reigned before he was assassinated, he managed to corrupt the land again. Though Josiah, his son, was a great king who sought to bring the people back to God, it was too late (2 Chron. 34:24-28). The shockingly evil and pervasive idolatry that came to characterize the people during the evil days of Manasseh had taken them so far away from God that there was no coming back for them. In the list of the "blessings and cursings" of the Law given in Deuteronomy, God had stipulated if they were unfaithful to Him, they would be punished by being sent into captivity (Deut. 28:36-37). He would keep that promise. In the pronouncement of judgment on the nation revealed in 2 Kings 21:11-15, this is specifically laid at the feet of Manasseh.

Lessons

Manasseh may have just been a really evil guy who was obsessed with worshiping every false god he could find in the most perverse ways, but it may be more complex than that. Despite his father's reforms, he was a product of a wicked culture. His reinstitution of idolatry may have been a combination of cultural pressures and political expediency. We too live in a world that surrounds us with voices calling for us to accept religious and moral pluralism. Sometimes it may seem easier and thus better to compromise a bit to avoid the consequences of being different. That's a road that leads much further than we would have ever imagined.

It would be nice if there was some assurance that the children of people of faith will turn out well. Though there are reasons to be optimistic that will be the case, there is no guarantee. What we can do is prepare as well as possible to be good parents, don't assume that our faith will automatically become our kids', realize everything we do has an impact, and never give up. After all, Hezekiah's son turned out well in the end.

Imagine putting an idol in the Temple and offering human sacrifices—including your own son. That's a terrifying degree of evil. It makes it even more amazing that God heard, rescued, and blessed him when he sought God with a penitent and humble heart. Such is the truly amazing grace of God. Regardless of where we have gone, there is always a way home.

While there is forgiveness for those who seek it, that forgiveness doesn't erase the consequences of our actions. Manasseh could not undo the damage that he did to the nation. He could not bring back those he had murdered. He could not change the influence he had on his son who followed in his steps. Even forgiven sins leave scars.

Questions

1. What would have been some of the advantages of training as a coregent? Can you think of any possible downside? What would it be like to be named king at 12 years old?

2. Make a list of the idolatrous practices in which Manasseh was involved.

3. Why would the way he was taken into captivity be especially humiliating?

4. Does it seem inevitable that he would repent? How else might he have reacted to the circumstances?

5. In what ways does the story have a happy ending? In what ways does it not?

Discussion

1. Discuss examples of different aspects of our world where we might feel pressured to conform to popular ideas. How are people who reject religious and moral pluralism often characterized?

2. Does God ever use difficult circumstances to help us learn lessons?

3. Is it easier for children to follow their parents' good examples or bad examples?

4. Explore the idea of there still being consequences for sin even when the sins are forgiven. How can we still suffer consequences for our own actions after we are forgiven? How might others continue to suffer consequences for the things we have done?

5. Manasseh was a man who zealously and violently acted in opposition to the will of God, but received grace and was forgiven. Can you find parallels with anyone in the New Testament? How does his case provide us with hope when we have sinned?

Esther

The book of Esther and her personal story are wonderful. She is a true heroine. It's a great story because of how she became a heroine. It wasn't because she was bitten by a radioactive spider or came from another planet. She became a heroine as she experienced a transformation of character that allowed her to rise to the occasion. (Quote box). She wasn't always a heroine. In fact, she wasn't always even a particularly "good" person, but she changed. Sadly, that's surprising to some because they learned a very sanitized and inaccurate version of the story that is of a complex young woman in very complex circumstances.

Context
The story took place during the days of a spoiled and petulant Persian king named Xerxes who decided to throw a six-month drunken bash to impress his allies and leaders in his court and entertain his people. During the revelry, he summoned his wife, Vashti, to show her off. She refused the summons and so angered and embarrassed him that he decided to replace her. In the process of all of this, he took his army to Greece and experienced a humiliating defeat. With all of this going on, he needed something to help him get his mojo back, and kings need queens. His advisors concocted a plan to find one that involved searching the empire for the most physically attractive women, bringing them to the capitol for an extended period of pampering, and then giving them one night with the king to see how they performed.

Enter Esther

She was a Jewish girl of indeterminate age under the guardianship of her older relative Mordecai. Physically, she fit the bill to be a candidate for the "queen audition," so she was chosen. The king's servant who was in charge of the young women liked her and gave her special treatment (Esther 2:9). During this year she hid the fact that she was Jewish (Esther 2:10). That would mean that under such strict supervision, she not only didn't tell anyone she was Jewish, but did not live as a Jew under the Law. She must have ignored the regulations concerning diet, holy days, ritual purity, etc., that set Jews apart from Persians. When her time came to spend the night with the king, she did so and so impressed him that he chose her to be queen. Spending the night with the king meant exactly what it sounds like it meant. After being chosen, she continued to conceal her nationality/faith (Esther 2:20). Perhaps she and Mordecai did this until she felt more secure in her position and safer, or perhaps it was because she assimilated into the culture and was rejecting her own culture. Regardless, we have seen nothing about her that should favorably impress us to this point.

Troubled apologists may jump in at this point and say, "But she had no choice!" Don't try telling that to Daniel and his three friends who risked death rather than conform to the pagan cultures in which they found themselves. Don't even try telling that to Vashti who maintained her integrity in the part of the story that included her.

Trouble Ahead

As time passes, the plot thickens, and the story becomes even more complex. Mordecai, who is perhaps the key figure in the book, uncovers an assassination plot and saves the king, but he is not rewarded (Esther 2:21-23). In the meantime, a cruel, petulant megalomaniac named Haman becomes the king's prime minister. Mordecai repeatedly refused to bow down to Haman, and this became an issue when it was pointed out to him by other court officials. During this time, it was also revealed that Mordecai was Jewish (Esther 3:2-4). Haman was so angered by this that he decided to plot genocide against the Jews (Esther 3:6). He presented his plan to the king in a way that concealed the specific identity of the people he wanted to destroy, assured the king that it would be helpful, and would put money in the treasury. The plan was that on a specific date the other people from the empire were to be permitted to kill their Jewish neighbors and take their possessions (Esther 3:8-13).

When the decree was issued Mordecai found out about it and realized that something needed to be done. While displaying mourning in a very obvious, public way, he went to the palace to alert Esther and call on her to act (Esther 4:1-2). When Esther learned that he was there and how he was dressed and behaving, she had clothes sent to him. Perhaps it was so that he would be allowed inside, but it seems more likely based on what we have seen from her so far and by his refusal to accept them that she was embarrassed by his behavior (Esther 4:4). The ensuing exchange of messages gave Esther the details of Haman's plan and the catastrophic consequences it would have for the Jewish people. She was the obvious person to try to intervene with the king.

Her response to these dire circumstances was, "All the king's servants and the people of the king's provinces know that for any man or woman who comes to the king to the inner court who is not summoned, he has but one law, that he be put to death, unless the king holds out to him the golden scepter so that he may live. And I have not been summoned to come to the king for these thirty days"(Esther 4:11).

To approach the king unsummoned was to risk death, and she was unsure of how he would respond to her since he had not called for her in a month. Despite the chilling danger her people faced, she was initially unwilling to put herself at risk. Her inactivity would make her complicit in the act if she failed to try to intervene. Her inglorious career as a Bible character has hit a new low.

A Hero Emerges

Mordecai's response was a veiled threat and warning that called her to rise to the occasion and make a difference (4:13-14). These words resonated with something that was probably buried deep inside her all of the time. Her response revealed a very different person was emerging.

"Go, assemble all the Jews who are found in Susa, and fast for me; do not eat or drink for three days, night or day. I and my maidens also will fast in the same way. And thus I will go in to the king, which is not according to the law; and if I perish, I perish" (Esther 4:16)

"If I perish, I perish." With these words, we see a change in her identity, focus, and priorities. She had been a person to whom and for whom everything had been done to that point (2:8,10,15, 20, etc.). She had been a passive observer of her own life. Suddenly, it's very different. Verse 16 is not simply an "okay, if I get killed, I get killed." While that's the focus of the text, it's more complex. She prefaces that courageous conclusion with a series of orders she issues to help ensure her success.

During the days of the fast, she was actively working out a complex and brilliant plan that included her approach to the king—a multi-staged party—and what she will do as it all unfolds (5:1-8). In all of this, she has owned her Jewish identity, prioritized protecting her people over her position and baubles, and risked her life. Surely, she had a heart that contained potential for goodness and was touchable. She had the potential to come up really big when the situation arose.

Her plan worked beautifully in every way. The leadership she had begun to provide continued as we see her role in successfully protecting her people across the empire and dealing severely with their enemies (Esther 8:1, 9:12-13,29-32).

Sidebar

The name of God is not mentioned, or even cleverly embedded, in the book. That does not mean his power and providence are not present on each page. He was constantly working behind the scenes in what is delightfully described as coincidence. I think this aspect of the book makes it especially helpful to us in our complex world because it reminds us that God is still working through people and circumstances to accomplish his purposes and keep his promises.

Lessons

As always, the most basic lesson is that an all-powerful and faithful God keeps his promises. He accomplished that then as he does now through his providential role in the lives of people and circumstances. This even includes being able to use the evil men choose to accomplish his will.

Esther is a wonderful example of someone who didn't seem to have a lot of potential to do something that mattered, and who had made enough questionable choices it would have seemed from a human perspective to have eliminated her from being part of God's plan. Yet once again we have seen how God can take, mold and empower weak, immature people with questionable pasts to allow them to be accepted by him and used for great service. Every one of us should be grateful for that.

One of the greatest problems we face in our world and perhaps in our own lives is selfishness. As our story demonstrated, this problem isn't new. We cannot allow our daily choices to be determined by what we like, we want, makes us happy, makes us feel good about ourselves, or even seems safer. Selfishness creates all kinds of problems and must be resisted. God expects us to care about those around us. Only when we do this are we imitating Jesus (James 3:16, Phil. 2:3-5).

We must not allow life to just "happen" to us. It's imperative that we grow up and take responsibility for our lives. It easy to make excuses and blame others, but growing up means taking ownership of our decisions. In the end, we will answer to God for them (2 Cor. 5:10).

The world tells us that power, wealth, fun, and security are the greatest things we can have. The world is lying to us. Unfortunately, when we listen, we find ourselves devoting our time, attention, and other treasure to their pursuit. What really matters is being a part of God's people dedicated to serving him. When Jesus tells us to take up our crosses daily and follow him (Luke 9:23), he didn't mean do it when it's fun, convenient, doesn't interfere with anything else we want to do, and doesn't cost too much. If there's not a cost, it's not a cross. We must be willing to give up the things the world tells us are most valuable to win the truly valuable crown.

Questions

1. Our text is filled with "coincidences" that are not really just coincidental. Identify some of these and think about how many different things had to come together for the story to unfold as it did.

2. What are some of the stipulations from the Law that Esther would have ignored to conceal her identity?

3. While your lesson gives a very general overview of the story, it leaves out a lot. What are some of the other details you find especially interesting and pertinent?

4. How does the text of 4:16 show Esther transitioning from being a very passive person to a much more proactive person taking responsibility for what was going on?

5. What role did the multi-day party play in Esther's plan?

Discussion

1. What do you think were the most difficult choices Esther had to make? Once she chose her path, did the choices become more or less challenging?

2. Can you think of some other Bible examples of God using even the evil that people did to accomplish his purposes? Did that exonerate them of accountability? Why or why not?

3. Do we ever find ourselves making excuses and blaming others for what we do? How do we overcome that?

4. Discuss some circumstances that actually do arise in our lives where we would need to find courage and risk some things that might be valuable to us. How do we prepare ourselves to "come up big" when that happens?

Peter

He may be one of our favorite characters not only for his wonderful character and personality, but also because we can so easily relate to his failures. He was a good guy trying to do the right things, and he often did, but other times he crashed and burned. He is the quintessential "Complex Character." We have so much data about him we will need to organize the material a little differently. Let's begin with a brief description and then look at a few specific personality traits that we will identify from various episodes in his life. After we see how these traits held both the potential for good and bad, we will find some lessons for our lives.

Peter was a professional fisherman on the Sea of Galilee (Matt 4:18). From various details about his work given throughout the gospels, we can reach some solid conclusions that help us paint a picture of him much more likely to be accurate than what you see in Renaissance-era paintings. He was a competent businessman, but he would have also been physically strong and agile. In all likelihood, he would have had a weather-beaten face from the sun and the wind. His hands would have been strong, calloused, scarred, and he might even have had a "roper's thumb."

Personality Traits
Passionate. Peter was clearly a very passionate person. Whatever he felt or did, he brought energy to it. He was "all in" when he made a decision. For example, he would say to Jesus that he had left all to follow him (Mark 10:28). While he was painting in bold strokes

(he did still have a house, boat, and wife—in no particular order), he had surely put following Jesus ahead of all of these things. In his discussion with Jesus during the "Last Supper," after Jesus finally convinced him that he should wash his feet, Peter wanted his hands and head washed as well (John 13:8-9). When Jesus foretold that the apostles would abandon him, Peter emphatically insisted that he would stay until the end (Matt. 26:35). Later, after he had denied Jesus, he was passionate in his shame and sorrow for his failure (Mark 14:72). He was 100%, full-speed, all-in in whatever he did whether he was properly informed or doing what was right or not.

Bold. Surely, he was a bold individual. His willingness to "put himself out there" was demonstrated in a variety of ways and settings. He had questions, and he wasn't shy to say that he wanted answers. While the entire group of disciples were struggling to understand much of what Jesus taught, Peter was willing to speak up and ask for an explanation (Matt. 15:15). He was also bold enough to speak and answer questions. It was he who answered Jesus' question by confessing that Jesus was "the Christ, the son of the living God" (Matt. 16:15-16). After the resurrection, he was willing to share this with a disconcerting and humanly inexplicable boldness (Acts 4:13).

When he thought the situation merited it, he was willing to make suggestions and offer advice. In his excitement at the Transfiguration of Jesus, he suggested that three booths be built—one each for Moses, Elijah, and Jesus (Mark 9:5). He made this suggestion because he actually had no idea what he should say (Mark 9:6). He was bold, and often it was good, but sometimes it was thoughtless and misguided.

Courageous. This is the trait we so often recognize in Peter, and for good reason. He showed great courage on many occasions. His response to seeing Jesus walking on the water was to ask if he could do so as well. He was courageous enough to get out of a perfectly good boat on the Sea of Galilee to walk to Jesus (Matt. 14:28-29). When the others all fled during the arrest of Jesus, Peter followed, though at a distance all the way to the court-yard of the house of Caiaphas (Mark 14:50-54). While we don't typically think of him showing any courage on this occasion, he showed more than those who simply ran away. He was showing courage by putting himself in harm's way. Most would have been nowhere near. When those who had killed Jesus ordered him to stop preaching the resurrection, his response was to say:

> "We must obey God rather than men. The God of our fathers raised Jesus, whom you killed by hanging him on a tree. God exalt-ed him at his right hand as Leader and Savior, to give repentance to Israel and forgiveness of sins" (Acts 5:29-31, ESV).

He had the courage to continue sharing that message until the day it cost him his life.

He was wonderfully courageous, except for those occasions when his courage failed. After he began to walk on the water to Jesus, he "saw the wind," got scared, and began to sink (Matt. 14:30). When confronted by a female servant in the High Priest's courtyard, he was so frightened that he began the three-part denial of Jesus (Mark 14:69-71). Even after the resurrection, his courage would fail on an occasion recorded for us. He was willing to eat and associate with the Gentiles until Jewish believers from the "circumcision party" came, and he was so afraid of them that he stopped what he was doing (Gal. 2:12).

His courage was such that he often put himself into dangerous situations that less courageous people would have never gone into. But problems arose when his courage was not properly based, or he lost focus.

Action

He was a man of action. While others might be planning, contemplating, or wishing, Peter was doing. When Jesus called him, he immediately left his nets and followed (Matt. 4:20). We may appreciate this more when we contrast his response with that of some others. While some would turn away from from jesus because of something he taught or make excuses for why they couldn't follow him when called, Peter was different. When Jesus called him, he acted.

In the previously discussed story of Jesus walking on the water, while the others might have been impressed, thought about how nice it would be to do that, or even wished they could, it was Peter who acted by requesting and actually getting out of the boat to do it (Matt. 14:28-29). During the arrest of Jesus, other disciples thought about resisting, and even asked if they should. It was Peter who actually acted and tried to kill a guy (Luke 22:49, John 18:10). Peter was truly a person of action, and that's a good thing if it is the proper action.

Strong Convictions

Peter demonstrated his strongly held convictions in numerous gospel narratives. In Acts 4, while speaking to the powerful and ostensibly knowledgeable religious leaders he spiritedly expressed his convictions that they were in the wrong, needed to change, and could only be saved through Jesus (Acts 4:11-12). On the Day of Pentecost, he told those gathered that they had murdered the Messiah, and the only solution for them was to be fully convinced of who Jesus was (Acts 2:22-23,36). At the gathering described in Acts 15, he powerfully argued against those who were trying to bind certain parts of the Law on Gentiles who had become Christians (Acts 15:10).

We saw in all of those incidents his strong convictions and the good it led him to do. However, he was also strongly convicted at times when he was wrong. When Jesus began washing the disciples' feet, Peter "knew" that the master washing the disciples' feet was inappropriate, and he expressed this strongly (John 13:8). After confessing Jesus to be the Son of God, he reacted strongly to Jesus telling them that he would suffer and be killed in Jerusalem. Peter "knew" that this was simply not right, and he rebuked Jesus for saying it (Matt. 16:22). (Please don't miss the irony of Peter taking Jesus aside to rebuke him, but in the rebuke referring to Jesus as "Lord.") When the Lord showed him the vision of the clean and unclean animals and told him to eat them, Peter "knew" that it was wrong to eat the unclean animals, so his initial response was "no" (Acts 10:14). It was great that he held strong convictions and was determined to live by them as long as his convictions were right. It also said much for his character that he was willing to change his convictions when he learned that he was wrong.

Resilient

Peter never quit. When most disciples were walking away from Jesus after his "bread of life" sermon, Peter, though likely as confused and troubled by it as the others said, "Lord, to whom shall we go? You have the words of eternal life, and we have believed, and have come to know, that you are the Holy One of God" (John 6:68-69, ESV).

Despite the shame he felt after denying Jesus, he didn't just give up. He showed up and had that difficult conversation where the Lord asked him three times if he loved him (John 21:15-17). After Paul publicly rebuked him for his hypocrisy, he didn't quit or become angry at Paul. When he wrote 2 Peter, he referred to Paul as "our beloved brother Paul" (2 Peter 3:15). When his own death was near, he told those he was writing to that he would keep working to teach and encourage them as long as he had life in his body (2 Peter 1:13-14). Peter realized that you don't lose the fight until you stop fighting, and he never did.

Lessons

Peter was a strong person with a strong personality. His personality traits helped him to do some wonderful things, but they also set him up for some colossal failures. The key to him doing well was having these traits properly harnessed. He did well when he was acting on accurate information, focused on the right things, trusting in the strength that comes from God, and exercising self-control. The same is true for us.

We need to be passionate people, but that passion must be for the right things, and that passion needs to be ruled by truth. We need to be bold, and that boldness needs to be in well-guided service. We need to be courageous, and the source of our courage needs to be confidence we have from the Lord. We need to be people of action, but we need to be sure that the things we do are things God wants us to do. We need to have strong convictions, and those convictions need to be based on truth, and we need to be educable when we are wrong.

Looking at Peter's life reminds us that failures sometime come to the best and strongest of people. These inevitable setbacks provide us opportunities to learn and grow if we have the right kind of hearts. Correcting and overcoming our mistakes allows us to grow stronger and be better prepared to assist others who are struggling. This is all predicated on us being humble enough to admit when we are wrong and listen to correction with a good attitude.

Through the hottest fires and continual pounding, iron transforms into the best steel and finally becomes the sharpest blade.

Questions

1. What did Peter mean when he told Jesus that they had left all to follow him? How can we leave all and still have it?

2. In the cases where Peter's courage failed, what do you think caused the failure?

3. How would you define "strong convictions?"

4. What might have made Peter so sure that Jesus would not be put to death?

5. Describe the conversation between Jesus and Peter from John 21:15-19.

Discussion

1. Why is it sometimes difficult to be "all in?" How can we combat that?

2. Are we ever unwilling to ask questions when we don't understand? If so, why?

3. Which trait of Peter's most impresses you? Why?

4. Which of the traits we discussed would you like to improve on in your life?

5. Why is someone who doesn't possess the character traits we have discussed unlikely to accomplish much?

Thomas

What do you remember about Thomas? Does he have a nickname you remember?

- Thomas was one of the original 12 apostles of Jesus, so we might be tempted to imagine he was exempt from the kind sof challenges we have been considering?

- Of the apostles who were not part of the "inner circle," he was one of the most often mentioned apostles.

- He obviously had some outstanding qualities, but at times he struggled.

- He is typically misunderstood and under-appreciated because his life is sometimes defined by one event.

- Recorded events paint a fascinating picture of contrasts in his life.

- This lesson gives us an opportunity to see what Jesus did in helping him resolve the complexities he faced.

   In short, he was a complex character in a complex world.

   We will look at several key events in his life and how he coped with them. That will afford us the opportunity to learn some lessons from his experiences.

Courageous Thomas
Though his name appears in the lists of apostles (i.e. Matthew 10:3), he isn't specifically identified during the course of a particular event

until quite late in the ministry of Jesus. Near the end of Jesus' life, he and the apostles are spending time in Perea (John 10:40). In part, this is because of the determined and known plan the Jewish leadership has to kill him. While there, word arrived from Bethany that his dear friend Lazarus was critically ill. When Jesus informed the group that he was planning to go back to Judea, the apostles questioned his decision by reminding him of the threat to his life (John 11:7). After some additional discussion, Jesus tells them they are going. At that point, Thomas spoke up and said, "Let us also go, so that we may die with him" (John 11:16, ESV).

Please realize, this is not a lofty platitude about a hypothetical situation. This is a man who, though he genuinely believes going to Judea will likely lead to his death, is so loyal to Jesus he is willing to go. When someone needed to speak up and demonstrate a willingness to follow, he did. Maybe we should have nicknamed him "Courageous Thomas."

Confused Thomas

The disciples struggled mightily with idea that Jesus would not only die, but he would do so willingly. Following the eating of their final Passover together, Jesus emphatically pressed them to grasp what would be happening over the following hours. As he worked with them to help them accept and process the information, they continued to struggle and be confused. Though surely not alone in his confusion, Thomas actually expressed his. He said to Jesus, "Lord, we do not know where you are going, how do we know the way?" (John 14:5, NASB).

Looking back from our perspective of knowing how the story played out, we may be confused by his confusion. We might be tempted to be critical of what we see as spiritual obtuseness. (After all, we are *never* spiritually obtuse!) That would be unfortunate.

The reality is that people of faith are sometimes confused and uncertain. People who genuinely love the Lord are determined to seek, work, think, pray, and meditate with dogged determination until they have done their best to "get it." He cared about what Jesus was saying and was not too proud to ask. We might say this was another demonstration of his courage. Being bold and humble enough to express a lack of understanding can require courage.

Absent Thomas

None of the disciples expected Jesus to be raised on the Sunday of the resurrection. The women went to the tomb to finish preparing the body for burial. When the tomb was empty, they thought the body had been moved. After Jesus began appearing to them, the other disciples were skeptical. Not expecting and even doubting the resurrection was the norm.

On the day of the resurrection, Jesus appeared to the disciples as a group. During this meeting, Jesus showed the disciples the wounds in his hands and feet (John 20:19). For whatever reason, Thomas was not with them at that gathering, so he did not see Jesus (John 20:24). In fact, by being absent from the disciples on that Sunday, he missed out on many things. He missed the opportunity to:

- Be with the other disciples to encourage and be encouraged.

- See his resurrected Lord.

- Learn more about how the crucifixion and resurrection fit into God's grand plan.

- Celebrate the resurrection.

By being absent, Thomas missed out on a lot!

Doubting Thomas

Finally, the nickname you have been waiting for. As we have already seen, all of the disciples were at some point and to some degree "doubters." When the apostles heard the account of the women, they did not believe them, and thought the message of the resurrection was an "idle tale" (Luke 24:11). Thomas earned this appellation for not believing the report of the disciples as a group. When, after seeing him on the day of the resurrection, they told Thomas they had seen the Lord, he replied, "Unless I see in his hands the mark of the nails, and place my finger into the mark of the nails, and place my hand into his side, I will never believe" (John 20:25, ESV). He not only doubted, but he placed it in very strong terms. Only both seeing with his eyes and touching with his hands the physical proof would convince him. He was so adamant about that he assured them he would "never" believe otherwise.

Later, in the ensuing discussion with the Lord, Jesus said, "Have you believed because you have seen me? Blessed are those who have not seen and yet have believed" (John 20:29, ESV). Whether the initial part of the quote was indeed a question or a statement of fact, the meaning is clear. He was afforded the incredible and rare privilege of personally seeing the resurrected Jesus. This qualified him for his role as an apostle. Jesus pronounced the greater blessing on the overwhelming majority of those who have believed over the last 2,000 years without having personally saw Jesus, but because they listened to the evidence for the resurrection and realized it was true.

Most of the facts we accept as true and operate based upon are things that either we have not or cannot empirically prove. Yet we accept these things based on the testimony of others we have reason to trust. That is reasonable on our part, as is coming to believe in the resurrection based on a careful examination of the historical evidence of the eye-witness testimony for it. Thomas was blessed with the opportunity to personally see Jesus while we have the greater blessing for coming to faith without that personal experience (John 20:29).

Believing Thomas

On the following Sunday, Thomas was with the disciples (John 20:26). Given his skepticism, it's perhaps a little surprising and impressive that he was there. His presence was rewarded by the appearance of Jesus. From reading the text, it seems that after a greeting Jesus immediately addressed him with the offer of experiencing the kind of proof he had demanded. Then, Thomas did believe.

Our initial reaction might be, "Well of course he did!" That's an understandable response, but before dismissing his response too hastily let's consider the response of some to other miracles. The gospels are filled with accounts of people who saw the power of God displayed in Jesus who, while being unable to deny the miracle, still refused to believe in Jesus. We need look no further than the response of the Jewish leadership to the raising of Lazarus from the dead as alluded to earlier in this lesson.

Those leaders, who were already determined to kill Jesus before he raised Lazarus were even more so after Lazarus was raised (John 11:53). Not only did they want to kill Jesus, but as a practical matter, they decided to kill Lazarus as well to remove the walking, talking proof of what Jesus had done (John 12:10-11). This verifies the surprising statement of Abraham to the rich man in Luke 16. The rich man felt that Law was inadequate so he had requested that Lazarus go back to warn his brothers not to follow in his steps to which Abraham replied, "If they do not hear Moses and the Prophets, neither will they be convinced if someone should rise from the dead" (Luke 16:31, ESV).

Worshiping Thomas

It does not appear that he actually needed to touch Jesus in order to believe. His response to seeing and hearing Jesus was a powerful and profound expression not only of faith but also of worship. Thomas said, "My Lord and my God!" (John 20:28, ESV). Thomas went from doubting to a powerful proclamation not only of the resurrection, but of its significance in proving the deity of Jesus. He is an example of someone honoring the Son as they honor the Father (John 5:23). He is addressing Jesus as his "Lord" and his "God." This expression of worship is personalized and intensified with the identification of God as "my." This astounding utterance of faith illustrates how powerful the evidence for the resurrection truly was.

Serving Thomas

The apostle Thomas was one of those addressed by Jesus shortly before he ascended when Jesus commissioned them to take the gospel to the world. These men would be able to tell the world about Jesus including that they had witnessed the fact of the resurrection. While the New Testament does not tell us where and how most of the apostles did this, there are other texts produced by early Christians that can help shed some light on this. Some traditions have Thomas preaching in India, while others indicate he may have preached in Parthia. Either or both are very plausible. Regardless of where, there is absolutely no reason to doubt that he did continue to serve his "Lord" and his "God."

The complex and challenging task of processing the words and actions of Jesus must have been daunting for not only Thomas but also the rest of the apostles. They needed to:

- Overcome the prejudices of the day.

- Deal with confusing angry opposition.

- Try to understand difficult teaching.

- Ponder incredible displays of miraculous power.

- Work on accepting the looming rejection and crucifixion.

- Deal with the rollercoaster of emotions around the arrest, crucifixion, and resurrection.

In a word, it was all complex. The detail provided in the text provides fertile soil from which to harvest important and practical lessons.

Lessons

Sometimes things get really tough, and dealing with fear isn't fun. Courage isn't a lack of fear but is doing what we should despite the fear. There are times when someone needs to speak up courageously like Thomas did in our story.

We won't always get it. We will struggle to understand certain questions, situations, and circumstances. When we find ourselves in that situation, we need to doggedly persist in trying.

Thomas missed out on a lot by not being there on that Sunday of the resurrection. We miss out on a lot when we miss the opportunity to gather with our spiritual family each Sunday as well.

We don't need to be gullible, but we need to recognize the validity of evidence that comes in the form of credible testimony. That evidence gives us good reason to believe in the resurrection of Jesus, and by extension, all he said and did.

When we have that knowledge of who Jesus is and what he did, we need to be willing to worship and serve him.

Questions

1. Were the religious leaders serious about killing Jesus? How do we know that?

2. Explain the answer Jesus gave to Thomas' question in John 14:6.

3. Why did the religious leaders want to kill Lazarus?

4. Explain Luke 16:31.

Discussion

1. In what type of circumstance might you have the opportunity to display courage like Thomas?

2. Are you ever unwilling to ask a question? If so, why?

3. What do we miss when we don't assemble with our spiritual family on Sunday?

4. Do you believe in the resurrection? What about the evidence convinced you?

5. Try to imagine how wonderful it was for Thomas when he saw Jesus. Now try to imagine how wonderful it will be to see him when he comes again.

Paul

If Peter was the person everyone can relate to, Paul may be the person no one can. He seems to have already had it together, and always gotten it right. While it might appear that way, the reality is more complex. We have so much information about Paul that it's necessary to group it in a special way for this lesson. We will start with a lot of good things about him, but not the good things you might expect. Next, we will be reminded of what he had been before he met the Lord. After that, we will look at some clues that his life as a Christian was not without its challenges.

Good Stuff

Where do you start when thinking about the good things from the life of Paul? It could be by looking at the fact he was chosen as an apostle, the numerous churches he "started," the portion of the New Testament he authored, or his martyr's death, but that's not how we will do it. Let's start by looking at some specific great attributes of Paul, and then see how those relate to other things.

Zeal

Fire, energy, and passion are all words that describe Paul's entire life. It was true of Paul the persecutor as well as Paul the preacher. He had a zeal for the Lord's word, work, and people. Upon being baptized, he immediately began to preach (Acts 9:20). When he went to Jerusalem, he immediately sought out the brethren there (Acts

9:26). As the years passed, he stayed the same. In the latter part of his life he had big plans for taking the gospel where he had not preached it before (Rom. 15:24). Just before his death, he was still eager to have access to the scriptures (2 Tim. 4:13). His zeal made him willing to sacrifice his comforts, rights, and resources. Perhaps no verse captures his attitude better than this:

> "I will most gladly spend and be spent for your souls. If I love you more, am I to be loved less?" (2 Corinthians 12:15, ESV).

The list of experiences he relates in 2 Corinthians 11:23-28 is staggering. He chose to give up personal safety and comfort to preach the gospel. He would not do things that would be a hindrance to the message. He gave up his right to be financially supported by the church in Corinth because it might limit his effectiveness (1 Cor. 9:9-22).

He was also someone who was kind, gentle, forgiving, and optimistic. When he described his work in Thessalonica, he could use the metaphor of a woman with a nursing child to describe the gentle and tender care with which he approached the work there (1 Thes. 2:7-8). When the circumstances arose that demanded he be very firm in challenging or condemning behavior, it was painful for him and was an expression of love (2 Cor. 2:3-4). After all he had done and sacrificed for others when he was being tried in Rome, everyone deserted him, but he forgave them (2 Tim. 4:16). Others preached the gospel because they thought that doing so would further endanger Paul, but his response was to rejoice that the gospel was being preached regardless of the motive (Phil. 1:12-18). It was these characteristics that allowed him to do the things in God's service like those previously listed.

At this point, you may be thinking, "yes, that's the 'perfect' Paul that I absolutely cannot relate to." The reality is more complex.

His Past

Before he was "the apostle Paul," he was "Saul of Tarsus." During that period of his life he violently persecuted Christians. His goal was simple. According to his own words, he did it in an effort to "destroy" the church (Gal. 1:13). From the stoning of Stephen until his trip to persecute Christians in Damascus was interrupted by the appearance of Jesus, he was relentless in his efforts to eradicate Christianity. What means did he use to accomplish this? He would enter the houses of Christians and drag them away (Acts 8:3). Other times, he would seek them out in synagogues. Those that were found were beaten and/or imprisoned. (Beatings were sometimes administered in the synagogue.) Sometimes these punishments were deemed inadequate, so Paul would be a willing participant in killing people for being Christians (Acts 26:10). He did not limit his efforts to Jerusalem and Judea. He pursued them to foreign cities as well (Acts 26:11). As chilling as this is, it was his efforts to frighten and torture Christians into blaspheming by renouncing Jesus that may be most disturbing. Though some efforts have been made to argue that he never succeeded, there is no real reason to believe this is true. It is difficult to imagine the terror that his name struck in the hearts of many Christians. It is no wonder that he would describe himself as having been the worst sinner (1 Tim. 1:15).

Many things impress us about Jesus appearing to him on his way to Damascus and his becoming a Christian. As we contemplate that, let's not overlook the incredible emotional trauma realizing what he had done must have caused him. To realize that he was not like an Israelite hero of old fighting against the enemies of truth, but that he was a murderer must have been terrible to process. His heart was filled with gratitude for the grace he had received (1 Tim. 1:12-14), but he never forgot how much pain he caused and harm he did to those who became his brethren. Try to imagine what it must have been like for him to assemble for the first time with the Christians in Jerusalem and see people he had caused to be beaten and thrown into prison. There were probably family members of those he had helped have killed there as well. That left him with a lot to overcome.

At this point you might say, "Well, okay. I get it. He had a lot of bad in his past, but after his conversion every day was great, he had no challenges, never got discouraged or experienced temptation. It's that Paul I can't relate to." I'm sure the real Paul would not be able to either. Paul got discouraged, had struggles, and faced temptations. Let's look his own description of some of these situations.

He got, on occasion, really, really discouraged.

> "For we do not want you to be unaware, brothers, of the affliction we experienced in Asia. For we were so utterly burdened beyond our strength that we despaired of life itself. Indeed, we felt that we had received the sentence of death. But that was to make us rely not on ourselves but on God who raises the dead" (2 Cor. 1:8-9, ESV).

It's hard to imagine being much more discouraged than that. He got past it, learned from it, and was strengthened by it, but he experienced it. He also experienced temptation.

> "But I discipline my body and keep it under control, lest after preaching to others I myself should be disqualified" (1 Cor. 9:27, ESV).

He doesn't tell us what these temptations were, but they were real. If he failed to give these temptations the "knockout punch" indicated by the word translated "discipline," he would fall into sin and lose his reward. Sometimes the very process of trying to save others puts one in a situation to face temptation (Gal. 6:1).

In another text he offers a clue as to what one of his challenges might have been. In 2 Corinthians 12 he describes a "thorn in the flesh" that he was given as a "messenger of Satan." Sometimes when we look at this text we see only things like lessons about prayer or suffering, or how to respond when we face difficulties, but we don't let the text tell us the purpose of the thorn and God's refusal to remove it. The answer to that question is given in verse 7.

> "So to keep me from becoming conceited because of the surpassing greatness of the revelations, a thorn was given me in the flesh, a messenger of Satan to harass me, to keep me from becoming conceited" (2 Cor. 12:7, ESV).

The thorn was to protect him from becoming conceited. I know that because he tells us that twice in one verse. Think about all that he had experienced, done, and accomplished. Is it surprising that this presented the real danger that he would become conceited? The danger was real enough that the thorn was given, and God refused to remove it and let him suffer, even though Paul asked him to three times. This was surely a challenge that he faced.

Paul was an amazing example of faith who did incredible things, but he was also someone with a horrible past who throughout his life had to deal with temptation, disappointment, and discouragement. Yes, he was another truly complex character.

Lessons

Paul's life is a most compelling proof that a horrifically bad past can be overcome, a person can be forgiven and put into God's service in a wonderfully productive way. Read the entire text of 1 Timothy 1:12-17 that I've already referenced a couple of times, and when you read the last verse, say, "Amen!"

Each success we face in this life comes with its own accompanying dangers. Satan knows all the angles and plays them.

To follow Paul's example and mix metaphors, we are never done with the battle until we cross the finish line. We will have plenty of time to celebrate when we are rewarded with our crown of victory. Until then, we must keep working until we "explode through the tape" (Phil. 3:13-14).

People's lives are often more complex than we realize. Whether it's because we are too self-centered to notice, or because they don't choose to share it, it's true. We all have a lot of stuff we deal with in this really complex world.

The last lesson from this lesson and all of these lessons is that everyone's experience is complex. That complexity not only includes discouragements, disappointments and other challenges, but it includes weaknesses and failures. That is the human experience. That is, of course, with one exception. That exception was Jesus. His life was complex in all of the ways we have described except for the last. He never failed. He never sinned. He never gave in. While his experience was such that it allows him to understand our weaknesses and be our sympathetic High Priest, his own sinlessness allowed him to die for our sins. (Heb. 4:14-16).

Questions

1. How much of the New Testament did Paul write? How many churches did he "start?"

2. How many times would you need to suffer shipwreck before you decided not to get back on a ship?

3. Describe in your own words what it must have looked and felt like when Paul and his companions would burst into the home of a Christian.

4. How would Paul's "thorn in the flesh" help protect him from conceit?

Discussion

1. When someone seems too perfect, is it difficult to like or learn from them?

2. How would Paul's character that we examined relate to the tangible things he accomplished? What can we learn from this about our service?

3. What do you imagine Paul feeling on that first occasion when he worshiped with the church in Jerusalem? Why is not putting our sin behind us after we are forgiven so dangerous?

4. Which character in this study surprised you the most? Which was the most helpful? Why?